Contents

		Page
Plan of the book		iv
Introduction		vi
Unit 1	Relationships	1
Unit 2	Adverts	11
Unit 3	Reading	24
Unit 4	Food	37
Unit 5	Language	46
Unit 6	Travel	57
Unit 7	Animals	71
Unit 8	Health	85
Unit 9	Jobs	99
Acknowledgements		112

PLAN OF THE BOOK

UNIT	TOPIC/ VOCABULARY AREA	SUBJECT	READING SKILLS	USE OF ENGLISH/ GRAMMAR POINTS
1	Relationships	Mother and son Father and daughter Lonely hearts	Text identification Skimming Vocabulary—meaning from context Scanning Intensive	Past simple Linking words Parts of speech
2	Adverts	Cars Electric toothbrush Security devices	Anticipation Vocabulary—meaning from context Scanning Text comparison Skimming	Prepositions Passives Irregular verbs Parts of speech Prefixes and suffixes
3	Reading	Anxiety Poor reading skills Reading speeds	Skimming Intensive Text comparison	Linking words Modal verbs Phrasal verbs Reported speech Tenses
4	Food	Restaurant Etiquette Pizza delivery	Text identification Skimming Intensive Vocabulary—meaning from context Scanning	Phrasal verbs Parts of speech Prepositions Conditionals Question forms
5	Language	Self-confidence Mother-tongue interference Grammar	Text identification Skimming Intensive Anticipation Vocabulary—meaning from context	Relative pronouns Conditionals 1 + 2 Tenses Parts of speech
6	Travel	Travelogue Informal letters and postcards Country walks	Skimming Intensive Scanning Text identification Vocabulary—meaning from context	Prepositions Punctuation Tenses Phrasal verbs
7	Animals	Squirrels Dogs Pets	Anticipation Skimming Vocabulary—meaning from context Intensive Scanning	Adverbs Parts of speech Tenses
8	Health	Alternative remedies Smoking Dental disease	Vocabulary—prediction Vocabulary—meaning from context Scanning Text identification	Parts of speech
9	Jobs	Nursing Detectives Sales assistant	Anticipation Skimming Vocabulary—prediction Intensive	Parts of speech Tenses

STUDY/ EXAM STRATEGIES	EXAM-RELATED TASKS		PAGE
Language revision Priority list	Multiple choice vocabulary Text gap-fill Transformation exercise	Dialogue completion Directed writing Word building	1
Analysing multiple choice distractors Grammar revision time	Multiple choice vocabulary Multiple choice comprehension Text gap-fill	Dialogue completion Directed writing	11
Extensive reading Using a dictionary	Multiple choice comprehension Expansion exercise	Multiple choice vocabulary Vocabulary and phrasal verbs	24
Keeping a study note book	Multiple choice comprehension Text gap-fill Vocabulary and phrasal verbs	Dialogue completion Transformation exercise Multiple choice vocabulary	37
Monolingual and multilingual classes	Multiple choice comprehension Text gap-fill Multiple choice vocabulary	Word building Expansion exercise	46
Dialogue writing How and where to study to reduce stress	Multiple choice comprehension Text gap-fill Dialogue completion Transformation exercise	Expansion exercise Vocabulary and phrasal verbs Multiple choice vocabulary	57
Familiarity with past exam papers Mock exams	Multiple choice comprehension Text gap-fill Transformation exercise Multiple choice vocabulary	Expansion exercise Directed writing Word building	71
Vocabulary— remembering and building	Text gap-fill Multiple choice comprehension Sentence transformation Vocabulary	Dialogue completion Directed writing Multiple choice gap-fill Expansion exercise	85
	Multiple choice comprehension Expansion exercise Word building Text gap-fill	Vocabulary and phrasal verbs Dialogue completion Transformation exercise Multiple choice vocabulary	99

Introduction

For students and teachers

How to use this book

Who is the book useful for?

This book has been written for students preparing for the Cambridge First Certificate examination. However, it will be useful for any learners of English at an intermediate or upper intermediate level who wish to develop their reading skills through a variety of interesting texts and exercises.

What does the book cover?

The book contains 27 authentic texts and a collection of tasks to help students prepare for Paper 1 (Reading) and Paper 3 (Use of English). The texts are grouped in threes around a theme (Unit 1 – Relationships, Unit 2 – Adverts, Unit 3 – Reading), thus enabling students to consolidate and recycle vocabulary and grammar as well as developing different reading skills. This book is not intended to be a complete grammar revision course, and while structures are indicated as linking with particular texts, students will need to revise and consolidate any points they are unsure of, with the help of a teacher and a good grammar book.

Is it necessary to follow the units in order?

It is advisable, though not essential, to do this because the aim of the book is to provide the student with progressive exam preparation. The book is designed in such a way that all the different question types found in Papers 1 and 3 are dealt with by the end of Unit 3. Units 3 to 6 continue the gradual build-up of reading skills and exam techniques. In Units 7 to 9 the student is given less guidance and assistance, and the emphasis is placed on more straightforward exam practice.

As the book is topic based, students and teachers may want to use a unit in order to focus on the particular theme and related vocabulary.

It is not absolutely necessary to work through every activity of every unit, but again the progressive nature of the units makes this advisable.

Can the book be used by a student working on his/her own?

Yes. The book is intended for class/group work, but can be used by students working alone and checking their answers as they go along. A full answer key is available on request from the publishers.

However, it is important to be very well disciplined about the time limits set for some of the activities. It is also important to have a good break (at least 15 minutes) after every hour or so of concentration.

Does the book involve only reading?
No. Each section begins with warm-up activities involving discussion and exchange of ideas, and the book is full of pair work, group work and discussion activities to provide variety and useful speaking practice.

The student is often instructed to work 'with a partner'. It is not advisable to work with the same partner all the time, and it is usually better to work with someone of a different nationality. It is also possible to work with more than one partner where appropriate.

Is it a teaching book as well as a practice book?
Yes. One of the most important characteristics of the book is the gradual build-up of various reading skills.

- **Skimming for gist**: this gives the student a general idea of the text and encourages quick reading and confidence.
- **Scanning for information**: in this type of exercise, students are encouraged to look for specific information quickly, rather than waste time reading every word.
- **Guessing meaning from context**: one very frequent problem for students is blocking at unknown words. The book includes many exercises designed to combat this, and to increase confidence and skill in this area.
- **Intensive reading**: multiple choice questions often contain many little traps for the unwary. Analysis of 'distractor' questions, and help on how to approach a text when faced with the need for intensive reading, will again build confidence and equip students with the necessary approach.

Students are also asked to work things out for themselves, which helps them to develop more autonomy than most exam books allow, and are guided towards learning strategies that best suit them.

Is it a good idea to use a dictionary?
Deriving meaning from context is an important exam skill. (You cannot use a dictionary in the exam.) However, it is equally important to check your answers in a good English-English dictionary, which will develop your reading skills and help you with word building.

Is it a good idea to use a grammar book?
The grammar points that come up here have been chosen because they are frequently examined in First Certificate papers. It is, therefore, important to research and practise thoroughly any grammar points that cause you problems as you are using this book.

Are the time limits important?
You may not at first be comfortable with the strict time limits. However, they are designed to help you develop the ability to read quickly through a text and get a broad idea of its contents. Working to the time limits will also help you to improve your reading speed. Remember that you have to read and work quickly in the exam.

Useful Addresses
UCLES (University of Cambridge Local Examinations Syndicate)
1 Hills Road
Cambridge CB1 2EU

BBC London Calling
P.O. Box 76
Bush House
Strand
London WC2B 4PH

London Calling is the programme journal of the BBC World Service. It contains a guide to the current transmission times and radio frequencies for your area.

English Teaching Information Centre
Central Information Service
The British Council
10 Spring Gardens
London SW1A 2BN

The British Council gives information on general and specialised courses in English as a foreign language.

ARELS-FELCO
2 Pontypool Place
Valentine Place
London SE1 8FQ

ARELS-FELCO is a professional association of private English language schools and organisations recognised as efficient by the British Council. The association produces a guide for foreign students called *Learn English in Britain with ARELS-FELCO*.

Unit 1 Relationships

Section A

10 SECONDS

1 The following text comes from a book called *The Growing Pains of Adrian Mole*. It is written in a particular style.
Look at it very quickly and decide if it is like

    a) a newspaper article.
    b) an entry in a diary.
    c) the script for a film.

Discuss your choice with a partner and give reasons.

Monday November 1st
  FULL MOON

After school I went to the hairdresser's with my massive mother. She didn't want me to go but she can't be allowed out of doors on her own, can she? Women are always having babies in phone boxes, buses, lifts etc. It is a well-known fact.

    Franco's is run by an Italian bloke. He shouted at my mother as soon as she got through the bamboo door. He said, 'Hey, Pauline, why you no come to see Franco once a week like before, heh?'

    My mother explained that she couldn't afford to have her hair done regularly now.

    Franco said, 'What foolish thing you say! Hair first, food second. You want your bambino to open his eyes and see an ugly mama?'

    I was astonished to hear the way he bossed my mother about, but for once she didn't seem to mind. He wrapped a sheet around her neck and said, 'Sit down, shut up, and keep still,' then he tipped her backwards and shampooed her hair. He told her off for having a few grey hairs and moaned about split ends and the condition. Then he dried her hair in a towel and made her sit in front of a mirror.

    My mother said, 'I'll just have a trim please, Franco.'

    But Franco said, 'No way, Pauline. I cut it all off and we start again.' And my mother sat there and let him do it!

    She also let him spray her bristle-cut hair purple and she paid him for doing it. *And* gave him a tip!

RELATIONSHIPS

2 Have you ever kept a diary? Why/why not? What kind of things did you write about? Discuss with your partner.

1 MINUTE

3 Now look at the text again and decide

　a) how many people there are.
　b) who they are (jobs/relationships).
　c) where they are.

4 Now read the text carefully and do the exercises that follow.

　a) How old is the writer? Give reasons to support your answer.
　b) Here are some statements about the writer's feelings towards his mother. Underline the words in the text that support them.

　　1 He doesn't like her new haircut.
　　2 He feels protective towards her.
　　3 He is surprised by her lack of resistance to Franco's ideas.

　c) Which picture best represents Adrian's mother after her visit to Franco's? Give reasons for your choice.

1　　2 　　3 　　4

5 Here is part of the text with some of the verbs missing. Fill the gaps without looking back at the text, using the following verbs: *moan shampoo tip make dry wrap tell*
Work with your partner and discuss the correct position and tense for each verb. Think of other suitable verbs that could be used apart from the ones given.

> He (1) .... a sheet around her neck and said, 'Sit down, shut up, and keep still,' then he (2) .... her backwards and (3) .... her hair. He (4) .... her off for having a few grey hairs and (5) .... about split ends and the condition. Then he (6) .... her hair in a towel and (7) .... her sit in front of a mirror.

Look at the text again to check your answers. Which tense is used, and why?

6 Match these words from the passage to the dictionary definitions.

a) massive (adj.)   1) very surprised
b) bloke (n.)   2) a small amount cut off
c) astonished (adj.)   3) send liquid through the air in small drops
d) trim (n.)   4) very large
e) spray (v.)   5) a man (informal)

Look the words up in your dictionary to check your answers.

7 Franco's English is good enough for him to run a successful business with English-speaking clients. However, it is not accurate enough to pass the Cambridge First Certificate. Here are some of the things he says. Can you correct them?

a) Why you no come to see Franco once a week like before ... ?
b) You want your bambino to open his eyes and see an ugly mama?
c) I cut it all off and we start again.

STUDY HINTS
Franco has particular problems with forming questions and the correct use of tenses. Discuss **your** grammar problems with a partner and look at these grammatical points that frequently come up in the First Certificate exam. You should pay particular attention to them as you prepare for the exam.

use of past tenses	when/while
passives	relative clauses (which/that/who ...)
conditionals (if ...)	although/in spite of/however
comparatives	question-forming
superlatives	since/ago/for
prepositions	too/enough
phrasal verbs	verb + infinitive/verb + -ing
reported speech	

RELATIONSHIPS

8 In Paper 3 of the First Certificate you will be given tasks like the one below. They are called 'transformation' exercises and are designed to test your knowledge of grammar.

Exam Practice

Finish each of the following sentences in such a way that it means exactly the same as the sentence printed before it.

EXAMPLE: 'Where is my husband?' Mrs Smith asked.

ANSWER: Mrs Smith asked ..*where her husband was*..................

a) I haven't seen her for six years now.

   The last time ....

b) He asked me if I wanted to dance.

   'Would ....

c) They got married in 1987.

   They've ....

d) You remembered to lock the door, didn't you?

   You didn't ....

e) They started living together more than 5 years ago.

   They've ....

f) She refused to go out until he apologised.

   'I ....

How many of the grammar points in **STUDY HINTS** appear in the transformation exercise above?
Discuss any problems you have with a partner and with your teacher.

RELATIONSHIPS 5

Section B

1 Where would you find this text (e.g. magazine, newspaper)? Discuss your answer with a partner and give reasons.

> Analysing my parents' failures, I decided that they had not wanted enough to be rich and successful; otherwise they could not possibly have mismanaged their lives so badly. I was torn between the desire to help them, to change their lives, to present them with some extraordinary gift, and the determination not to repeat their mistakes. I had a superstitious belief in my power to get what I wanted, which events seemed to confirm; after months of dogged studying I won a full college scholarship. My father could barely contain his pride in me, and my mother reluctantly yielded before my triumph and his.

2 Look at the text again and decide

  a) how many people there are.
  b) how they are related.

3 Here are some statements about the text. Decide which are true (√) and which are false (×). First do the task on your own. Then check and discuss your answers with a partner.

  a) The writer is an intelligent and successful student.
  b) The writer's parents are successful people.
  c) The writer's parents have wasted their opportunities to be rich and successful.
  d) The writer resolves not to repeat their mistakes.
  e) The parents' failure is due to lack of ambition.

4 Can you complete this short paragraph, using the appropriate linking words from the box below?

The writer is an intelligent and successful student. Her parents, (1) ...., have wasted their opportunities to be rich and successful. The writer decides their failure is due to a lack of ambition (2) .... is determined not to repeat their mistakes. (3) ...., she also feels she ought perhaps to help them.

> then   because   on the other hand
> so   but   although   and   however

6 RELATIONSHIPS

5 Here is another extract from the same book. Half the dialogue is missing. Working with a partner, read the text and fill the gaps with the following words spoken by the writer:

a) 'That's what I'm planning to do.'
b) 'I'll pay you room and board if you like. I'll work nights.'
c) 'I'm old enough to do as I like.'
d) 'Everyone drinks in college.'
e) 'You've got no right to order me around. I'm paying for my own college education.'
f) 'I heard you.'
g) 'I don't see why not.'

We drank to the future. Father poured two fingers of whiskey for himself and a wineglass of sherry for Mother. As he turned away I recklessly poured some whiskey for myself.

'You're not drinking whiskey,' Father said.
(1) ....
I quickly swallowed half a shot.
'I just said you're not to drink whiskey.'
(2) ....
The glass was still in my hand; I took another swallow.
(3) ....
'You're not in college, you're in your home.'
'Leave her alone,' Mother warned.
(4) ....
I said.
'I don't care how old you are. While you're under this roof you'll do as I say.'
(5) ....
I held the glass to the light, then drank the last of it.
'Esther, that's enough!' Mother said.
(6) ....
'Get out of here!' Father shouted.
(7) ....
I said calmly. I felt on fire and my legs were shaking. I'm free, I thought exultantly, I'm on my own.

RELATIONSHIPS

Section C

10 SECONDS

1 Where would you find a text like this?

- **PROFESSIONAL, 49** (looks much younger), fit, bearded, 5'8", Aquarius, W.2. Seeks a good but not too good woman. Dinner, perhaps? Box N672
- **VERY ELEGANT LADY,** warm-hearted, easy-going, 45, 5'7", dark. Seeks tall, attractive male, intelligent with sense of humour and style. Photo please and telephone number. Box N563
- **ENORMOUSLY ATTRACTIVE, STYLISH FEMALE,** 30's, slim, bright, well-travelled. Wishes to meet single, good-looking, successful man for relationship or more? Photo ensures a reply. Box N633
- **I'M HERE. COME AND GET ME.** Female, 40-ish and so much to give. Box N677
- **EXECUTIVE RUSSIAN LADY,** 37, world-travelled, extrovert, excellent sense of humour with high standards. Would like to meet gentleman of taste to enjoy operatic nights. Box N412.
- **WHY** is it so difficult to meet stimulating people in London? Good-looking female graduate, 24, neither without friends or beauty wants to meet intelligent interesting rugby player. Photos a must. Box N587
- **NURSE,** 25, bearded, 5'2", honest, reliable, passionate. Seeks cuddly belly dancer with enchanting eyes. Photo/telephone. Box N536
- **SHY, WITTY PILOT, 27.** Seeks amusing, beautiful lady for meaningful relationship. Photo please. Box N681
- **STUNNING ACADEMIC, 37,** needs saving from her well of loneliness. Box N294
- **MALE** (5'3", 38) professional, successful, handsome and generous. Seeks beautiful woman for friendship, country walks, conversation and weekends away. Box N786
- **AFFECTIONATE FEMALE, 38,** in South London seeks sensible soulmate and heart-shaped boxes of chocolates. Box N499
- **ATTRACTIVE, LOVING LADY (35)** wants independent man to share the good things in life. Box N579
- **LONELY, AFFECTIONATE GENTLEMAN** seeks delightful lady up to age 50. Any race, colour, creed or status. Box N678
- **ROMANTIC, ELDERLY GENT** seeks well-preserved, amusing and intelligent lady (60+) for tea and cakes by candlelight. Box N471
- **PRINCE CHARMING** in rural Kent. Romantic, compassionate, penniless Englishman (36) seeks princess for everlasting love. Interests: music, cricket, horses. Photo essential. Box N559
- **ATTRACTIVE, AFFECTIONATE, RETIRED LADY** seeks humorous, sprightly, mature man for companionship and chess. Tel. no. ensures reply. Box N487
- **MALE 32, CUDDLY,** sincere, ordinary. Seeks lonely lady. Age and figure immaterial. Box N873
- **YOU** are tall, slim and elegant with a heart of gold. I am tall, broad and 42 with a boat. Come and sail the seven seas with me. Photo and tel. Box N653
- **MALE 27,** warm-hearted and loving. Music teacher. Seeks slim, cheerful female. Box N329

2 Look at the text again and put a circle around the two adverts which you might reply to. Discuss your choice with a partner.

3 Find ten words or expressions from the text which describe appearance (e.g. attractive), and ten which describe character (e.g. affectionate).

4 Using some of the words and expressions from the text,

      either: a) write your own personal ad.
          or: b) write an ad. for a member of your group.

(Remember: each word costs £1.10)

5 Here are five people looking for partners. Decide which ads they should try replying to and give your reasons. There could be more than one possibility. Do the task on your own, then discuss your choices with a partner.

Sally: 30, slim, gentle, popular. 5'8". Feeling lonely. Has a good job with a bank.

John: 50, divorced with grown-up children. Successful and sophisticated businessman. Bearded and very handsome.

Ann: Late thirties, a little overweight, loving and generous. Hates TV and pop music.

Mike: 39, muscular. Heavy smoker and drinker. Loves parties and having a good time. Irresponsible and lazy.

6 In Paper 3 of the exam you may be asked to complete a short paragraph justifying your choices. Look at these two possibilities and decide which is better. Discuss your choice with a partner.

a) Sally must write to X. This nice guy is good for Sally.

b) Sally should try writing to X. They are both tall, slim, educated people. He is seven years older than she is but sounds very nice.

Now write one or two sentences to justify your choices for John and Ann.

7 Here are four adjectives from the text:

good-looking   attractive   beautiful   handsome

They have very similar meanings but are not perfect synonyms.

a) Can you explain the difference in meaning in the following examples?

　　1 a beautiful woman/a handsome woman
　　2 a good-looking old man/a beautiful old man

b) Some adjectives are associated with certain nouns and not with others. Can you decide which of the above four adjectives cannot be used with the following nouns?

　　1 baby   2 building   3 suggestion   4 meal

8 In Paper 1 of the exam you have to complete 25 sentences with one of a choice of four words. Although at first sight it seems that all four are suitable, there is only one that is correct. Look at this example:

We gave the youngest child a big .... teddy bear for Christmas.
A caring   B easy-going   C affectionate   D cuddly

People, animals or toys that have the quality of making you want to hold them close and show your affection to them are 'cuddly'. The other three adjectives here suggest some form of action, of which teddy bears are not capable. Therefore D is the only possible answer.

Exam Practice

Choose the word which best completes each sentence.

1   Isn't she beautiful? She's so tall and ....
    A slim   B thin   C skinny   D narrow

2   Whatever you do, don't mention the divorce; he's still very ....
    A sensible   B sensitive   C sensual   D serious

3   Mrs Jones felt so .... after the death of her husband and with all her children living in Australia.
    A solitary   B insulated   C solo   D lonely

4   I have such a(n) .... boss; she always gives me the day off and a big bunch of flowers for my birthday.
    A intelligent   B clever   C wise   D thoughtful

9 Now complete this table. The first one has been done for you.

NOUN	ADVERB	ADJECTIVE	OPPOSITE
intelligence	intelligently	intelligent	unintelligent
			irresponsible
sincerity			
	humorously		
passion			
	honestly		
		sensitive	
		reliable	

How many different ways do you know of forming the adjective from a noun? How many different ways do you know of forming the opposite of an adjective?

RELATIONSHIPS

10 You will find it easier to use a dictionary and to understand your teacher if you know what different parts of speech are (nouns, adverbs, adjectives, etc.).

You will find this awareness particularly useful for one of the questions in Paper 3 of the exam, which requires you to complete a sentence using the appropriate form of the word given at the end.

Look at the following example:

I didn't like the office much because the people were ....   FRIEND

Friend is a noun, but an adjective is needed to describe the people. However, **friendly** does not fit with the negative idea expressed in the context, so we have to change it to **unfriendly**.

I didn't like the office much because the people were *unfriendly* .

To do these exercises successfully you need to
   a) decide on the part of speech needed.
   b) decide whether the word needs to be positive or negative.

Exam Practice

Fill each blank with a suitable word formed from the word in capitals.

a) She listened to my problems very ....   SYMPATHY

b) I was upset by his .... ; he hardly noticed how unhappy I was.   SENSITIVE

c) He's such a caring person – full of .... and affection.   WARM

d) She'll never agree to go out with me. The situation is ....   HOPE

e) I'm fed up with superficial relationships. I'm looking for a deep and .... one.   MEAN

Unit 2 | Adverts

Section A

1 Look at this sentence and photograph. Where would you find them?

DRIVE ACROSS LAKE HORNAVAN
AND YOU LEARN A THING OR TWO ABOUT BRAKES.

12 ADVERTS

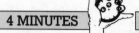 **2** With a partner, discuss what information the advertisement will probably contain. Write down 15 words you think the advertisement will use and group them according to whether they are nouns, verbs, adjectives or adverbs.

4 MINUTES

3 Here is the advertisement. As you read it, check your predictions. Then find the words which mean the same as:
   a) place (n.)
   b) little by little (adv.)
   c) divided (v.)
   d) sending liquid through the air in small drops (v.)
   e) metal made by mixing metals together (n.)

In the winter it enjoys three hours of sunlight a day and arctic temperatures that hover around the minus 40 mark.

To us, literally the frozen wastes. To the Rover test drivers, a kind of paradise. Solid ice, sixty four kilometres of it, and just the spot to put the ABS braking system on the Rover Vitesse through its paces.

First, our drivers test the brakes on a surface of hard packed snow on top of ice. Both car and brakes are pushed to the limit as stopping distances are gradually reduced.

Then the car is driven at high speeds on a split surface. Half ice, half false tarmac. (The false tarmac being created by spraying a mixture of water and gravel on the ice.)

Once the ABS system is tuned to its optimum and the cars are steering along the straight and narrow as well as round the bends, it's off to the next test.

The Austrian Tyrol maybe for yet more brake tests. The California desert for hot weather trials. Or even to glamorous Warwickshire, home of Rover's Gaydon proving ground.

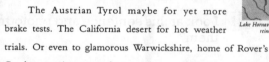
Lake Hornavan, Northern Sweden. Home to elk, reindeer and Rover test drivers.

That's where the 24 valve, 2.7 litre, V6 Vitesse engine, unhampered by speed limits, is really allowed to perform. 0-60 in 7.6 seconds. Top speed, 140 mph.

Small wonder then that the Vitesse comes with up-rated gas dampers, ultra low profile tyres, alloy wheels and sports suspension.

As well, of course, as all the comfort and refinement you'd expect from a Rover.

The Rover Vitesse Fastback. We've put it to the test.

Now it's your turn.

4 Exam Practice

In this exercise, choose the word which best completes each sentence, and then look back at the advertisement to check your answers.

1. Both car and brakes are pushed .... the limit.
   A at   B for   C to   D along

2. Then the car is driven .... high speeds.
   A in   B to   C at   D on

3. Small wonder that the Vitesse comes .... up-rated gas dampers.
   A on   B for   C in   D with

4. As well, of course, ... all the comfort and refinement you'd expect from a Rover.
   A with   B as   C to   D in

5

Read the text again and write four questions which check comprehension. Ask another student your questions and answer his/hers.

Were your questions similar to your partner's?
How? Discuss.

6

Comprehension is checked in the First Certificate exam by means of multiple choice questions. Only one of four possibilities is correct. The other three are called distractors. They are designed to distract you from the truth.

Multiple choice questions are designed to make marking quick and easy. They are not designed to help you; quite the opposite. They are often full of little traps.

Here is an example.

Decide if each answer is correct, partly true or rubbish.

The brakes on the Rover Vitesse Fastback are tested
A on five different surfaces.
B on at least five different surfaces.
C on two different surfaces in Sweden.
D by drivers from four different countries.

Tests take place in Sweden (see map), first 'on a surface of hard packed snow on top of ice' and then 'on a split surface'. C is therefore correct. Three other test areas are mentioned (the Austrian Tyrol, California and Warwickshire), but the use of the words 'maybe' and 'or' tells us that not all of them are used. A and B are therefore only partly true.

D is rubbish because although four different countries are mentioned, the text tells us nothing about the nationalities of the drivers.

7 Look at these two sentences. What grammatical construction do they have in common?

> Both car and brakes are pushed to the limit ...
> Then the car is driven at high speeds ...

Both sentences use the passive.

In Unit 1, page 4, some examples were given of the grammatical changes that have to be made in transformation exercises. The passive is often tested in these exercises.

Use the Rover 800 Series text to help you with the first two pairs of sentences in the following transformation exercise, and then do the others.

a) The drivers gradually reduce stopping distances.
   Stopping distances ....
b) We really allow the engine to perform.
   The engine ....
c) First, our drivers test the brakes on a surface of hard packed snow.
   First, the ....
d) We've put it to the test.
   It ....
e) We spent a lot of time trying to get things right.
   A lot of ....
f) You will find more examples of this kind of exercise in the exam.
   More examples ....

8 Here is a table of the most commonly used irregular verbs in English. The top part has been filled in correctly, but the bottom part is incomplete and some of the entries are wrong. Working with a partner, try to complete and correct the bottom part of the table.

Compare your answers with those of the rest of the group.

ADVERTS

VERB	PAST SIMPLE	PAST PARTICIPLE	VERB	PAST SIMPLE	PAST PARTICIPLE
be	was	been	have	had	had
become	became	become	hear	heard	heard
begin	began	begun	hold	held	held
break	broke	broken	keep	kept	kept
bring	brought	brought	know	knew	known
buy	bought	bought	leave	left	left
catch	caught	caught	let	let	let
choose	chose	chosen	make	made	made
come	came	come	put	put	put
do	did	done	read		
drive	drove			read	read
eat			run	ran	ran
	ate	eaten	see		saw
fall	fell	fallen	send		sent
feel			set	set	set
find	found		sit	sit	sit
get			stand		
give			take		taken
go			tell		
grow		grown	think	thonk	thunk

It is a good idea to keep your own table of the irregular verbs that cause you problems and add new ones to it as they come up.

Section B

INTERPLAK®.
AT LAST, A *GENUINE* TECHNOLOGICAL BREAKTHROUGH IN HOME DENTAL CARE.

▶ Forget any ideas you may have of conventional electric toothbrushes. Interplak – the revolutionary home dental care system from the USA – operates on a completely new principle. *It's the only domestic dental cleaning system that we've encountered which reaches the places where plaque forms.* And plaque is the major cause of gum disease.

Unlike any other type of toothbrush, electric or manual, Interplak's brush head does not move. Instead, its purpose-designed bristle tufts rotate at 4200 revolutions per minute – actually cleaning *between* the teeth and *below* the gumline, where plaque gathers and conventional brushing can rarely reach.

Five independent studies have shown that using Interplak is significantly superior to conventional brushing. *One American university found that the use of Interplak led to an average of almost 99% plaque-free surfaces.* (Manual brushing led to 50%.)

Interplak: at last, a technological breakthrough

The key to Interplak's remarkable effectiveness is its unique, patented brush head. The soft bristles in each tuft vary in length, and are gently tapered to provide contact with all surfaces. The long ones reach into crevices, the shorter ones scrub outer surfaces. Each tuft *rotates*, reversing direction 46 times a second and slightly lengthening and shortening.

Teeth are thoroughly cleaned…the lengthened tufts' thrusting movement dislodges trapped food particles…gums are gently massaged to make them healthier and firmer. Ordinary toothbrushes have a simple 'sweeping' action – bristles jam together, often missing the areas where Interplak can reach. Yet Interplak is gentle: its bristles are four times softer than those of an ordinary toothbrush.

Since Interplak's introduction, several Central London dental practices have decided to recommend it to patients, with a further 150 (including Harley Street practices, dental hospitals and government authorities) registering interest.

Family dental care – for a lifetime

Interplak is a rechargeable cordless unit, measures 10½" long and weighs 8 oz. Its on/off switch provides three cleaning speeds. The unit is engineered to the very highest standards and completely safe in water. When you're not using it, the unit simply trickle-charges in its recharging base, providing up to 20 minutes of continuous use (more than enough for the average family brushing twice a day).

Two colour-coded interchangeable heads are also included; additional heads for the rest of the family are also available for just £12.95. Each head lasts up to two years! Dentists agree that prevention is the best treatment for dental problems. Interplak's price is a small investment for the years of dental care it can provide for you and your family.

Complete with 12-month comprehensive warranty.

TOSET 1 Interplak	**£89.95**
Additional brush heads (each)	
TOHER1 (Red)	
TOHEY1 (Yellow)	**£12.95**

Interplak® is a registered trade mark of the Dental Research Corporation.

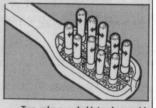

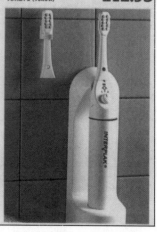

ADVERTS 17

2 MINUTES

1 The advertisement opposite has a distinct style.

Read the text quickly and decide if the advertisement has been designed to show that Interplak is
  a) extremely good value for money.
  b) fun and easy to use.
  c) a technically precise instrument.
  d) unlikely to electrocute its users.

Discuss your choice with a partner and give reasons.

2 Find three things this advert has in common with the one on page 12, e.g. use of pictures.

3 Exam Practice

Here are two multiple choice questions. Try to do them on your own and then compare your answers with a partner's.

1   Interplak, the revolutionary dental care system from the USA,

  A   cures gum disease.
  B   cures gum disease better than ordinary tooth brushes.
  C   removes some of the plaque from your teeth.
  D   can remove most of the plaque from your teeth and gums.

2   Interplak is recommended by

  A   the Government and some London dentists.
  B   some dentists in central London, although the Government and 150 other institutions are interested.
  C   many dentists in central London, although 150 other institutions are interested.
  D   some London dentists.

4 Look at the words printed in the table below and then look back at the text to see how they are used. Then complete the table.

NOUN	VERB	ADJECTIVE	ADVERB
forgetfulness	forget	forgettable / forgetful	forgetfully
			completely
	clean		
			significantly
direction			

18 ADVERTS

Using prefixes and suffixes (un-, in-, dis-, -less, etc.), find the opposite or negative form of the adjectives in the table, e.g. forgettable – unforgettable.

Now do the same for these adjectives:
honest responsible careful useful legal

5 The first paragraph of the text has been written below, with spaces above some of the words. Can you find a suitable alternative for each of the spaces? For example, 1 (Forget) – Give up, Disregard, Ignore.

(1) .... any ideas you may have of (2) ....
    (Forget)   (conventional)
electric toothbrushes. Interplak – the (3) ....
                                                (revolutionary)
home dental care system from the USA – (4) ....
                                                    (operates)
on a (5) .... new principle. It's the only
    (completely)
(6) .... dental cleaning system that we've
    (domestic)
(7) .... which reaches the (8) .... where
    (encountered)   (places)
plaque (9) ....
          (forms)
And plaque is the (10) .... cause of gum disease.
                         (major)

6 On page 6 in Unit 1, you were given the words of one speaker in a dialogue and were asked to use them to complete the dialogue. You may be asked to do a similar question in Paper 3 of the First Certificate exam, but you will have to supply the words of one speaker yourself. Always make sure that questions and answers correspond exactly.

Exam Practice

Imagine you have bought an electric toothbrush. You discover that it doesn't work so you take it back to the shop.
Now complete the dialogue.

20 ADVERTS

Section C

45 SECONDS

1 Here are some more advertisements. Work with a partner to match the texts to the pictures.

1

Instant guard dog protection

Prowlers would think twice before approaching a home protected by a vicious guard dog – and this ingenious alarm is virtually indistinguishable from the real thing. Just plug the Boston Bulldog alarm into a mains socket and position it near a door or window and it will detect any loud noise and set off a realistic bark that lasts for almost a minute before switching itself off. It can also be used as a 'panic button' if you hear noises outside yourself. 240 volts AC only.
Boston Bulldog £44.95 E219

2

There's always someone in

Cost-effective ideas in home security are always worth looking at, and a simple way to deter burglars is to make them think there's someone at home. The Sensor Light will turn on automatically when it gets dark and off again at dawn. The Random Sensor Light does the same but also goes off and on intermittently. Both plug into standard bayonet light sockets and have manual override.
Sensor Light £12.95 E210
Random Sensor £18.95 E211

A

3

Your personal security guard

Ease your worries about the rising crime wave. The Quickguard alarm will protect your property from thieves instantly. It can be used either on your car or anywhere in the home to deter intruders and act as a highly effective burglar alarm. A sensitive motion detector inside the Quickguard will react to the slightest movement of your car, your house door or window – and immediately send out a high pitched alarm signal of 100 decibels. Quickly installed on the car exterior or inside under the dashboard, or on any door, windowframe or object in your home. The Quickguard is simple to operate, has an entry and exit delay and can only be deactivated with the special key provided. It measures only 3.3" x 3.3" x 1.7", so it's easy to hide. Takes one 9 volt battery, not included.
Quickguard £12.95 E212

4

Hide your assets

With nearly a million house burglaries every year in Britain, the Strongpoint Mark 2 is a highly effective, yet low cost way to keep your cash, jewellery, credit cards etc. secure from intruders. Developed with the help of Crime Prevention Officers and Master Locksmiths, it looks like an ordinary domestic power point. But concealed behind it is a strongbox with plenty of room to hide all your valuables. Simply installed in any cavity wall with a minimum 5½" depth.
Strongpoint £24.95 E215

B

C

D
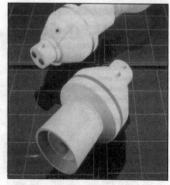

2 Where would you find advertisements like these?

ADVERTS

3 Exam Practice

*Fill each of the numbered blanks in the following sentences taken from the texts. Use only **one** word in each space. Then look back at the advertisements to check your answers.*

Prowlers would think twice before approaching a home (that was) protected (1) .... a vicious guard dog ...

It can also be used (2) .... a 'panic button' if you hear noises.

It can be used either (3) .... your car or anywhere (4) .... the home ...

The Quickguard is simple to operate ... and can only be deactivated (5) .... the special key ...

(It was) Developed (6) .... the help of Crime Prevention Officers ...

(It can be) Simply installed (7) .... any cavity wall ...

4 On page 8 in Unit 1 you had to justify some choices that you made. This time you have to go into more detail.

Look back at the advertisements for security devices. Which one would each of these people choose, and why?

a) John Brown   21 years old   A student

b) Sally Perkins   86 years old   A widow living on her own

c) Charles Oldfield 32 years old   A doctor working long, irregular hours

Discuss your ideas with a partner and then write a paragraph of about 60 words for each person.

John Brown would buy the Strongpoint Mark 2. He probably doesn't have a lot of money and wouldn't be able to afford ....
....

Sally, on the other hand, ...
....

The best thing for Charles ....
....

22 ADVERTS

5 When completing the type of exam question below, remember that words with very similar meanings are used differently, and that you must look carefully at the grammatical construction of each sentence before making your choice.

Choose the word or phrase which best completes each sentence.

1 They .... us to advertise on television.
   A suggested   B arranged   C proposed   D advised

2 Business is always looking for ways of .... its profits.
   A making   B growing   C increasing   D blowing up

3 This must be the best commercial I've seen ....
   A ever   B up to   C so far   D until

4 TV commercials are rarely long .... for people to get bored.
   A through   B enough   C time   D in order

5 A lot of people .... advertising for the rise in the number of young smokers.
   A accuse   B charge   C blame   D consider

6 In today's newspaper it .... that oil has been discovered off the west coast.
   A advertises   B notices   C writes   D states

7   The agency has a good .... for the quality of its advertising.
    A   reputation   B   character   C   respect   D   knowledge

8   We can't .... on a name for the product.
    A   decide   B   conclude   C   assent   D   consent

9   Don't buy that make of car. It's not ....
    A   confident   B   reliable   C   dependant   D   trusting

10 I was forced to .... down on the number of newspapers I advertised in because of rising prices.
    A   get   B   turn   C   pull   D   cut

STUDY HINTS

Set aside a period of time every two or three days for grammar revision and practice. 20–30 minutes is enough. (*Never* concentrate for more than an hour on new things.) During that period look at and practise *one* grammar point only.

The important thing is to do regular but small amounts of revision.

Unit 3 Reading

Section A

1 MINUTE

1 Here is an extract from a book called *Reading*, by Frank Smith. Skim the text and decide whether the book was written for

    a) children.
    b) psychologists.
    c) students of Russian literature.
    d) someone else. (Who?)

Discuss your choice with a partner.

Two words of advice

This book is intended to be practical, despite its range over a variety of theoretical disciplines. So perhaps I might conclude this first chapter with a couple of practical hints for the reader concerning the rest of the book.

  First, relax. Anxiety about being able to comprehend and remember can make any reader functionally blind. You may not realize that anxiety has this effect, but the more you are concerned about reading this book the less you are likely to comprehend it. Try to *enjoy* the book, put it aside for a while if you are bored or confused, and leave your brain to take care of the rest.

  And my second helpful hint is that you should not try to memorize anything you read in this book. The effort to memorize is completely destructive of comprehension. On the other hand, with comprehension the memorization will take care of itself. Your brain has had longer experience than you can recall in making sense of a complex world and in remembering what is important.

My two words of advice are exemplified in what I call the Russian Novel Phenomenon. Every reader must have experienced that depressing moment about fifty pages into a Russian novel when we realize that we have lost track of all the characters, the variety of names by which they are known, their family relationships and relative ranks in the civil service. At this point we can give in to our anxiety, and start again to read more carefully, trying to memorize all the details on the off chance that some may prove to be important. If such a course is followed, the second reading is almost certain to be more incomprehensible than the first. The probable result: one Russian novel lost forever. But there is another alternative: to read faster, to push ahead, to make sense of what we can and to enjoy whatever we make sense of. And suddenly the book becomes readable, the story makes sense, and we find that we can remember all the important characters and events simply because we *know* what is important. Any re-reading we then have to do is bound to make sense, because at least we comprehend what is going on and what we are looking for.

2 Exam Practice

Read the text again and answer these multiple choice questions.

1   The book advises readers to

    A   sit in comfortable chairs.
    B   try to remember the important parts.
    C   stop if they get bored.
    D   read only the things they enjoy.

2   Frank Smith says everyone

    A   has read a Russian novel.
    B   should read a Russian novel.
    C   reads a Russian novel twice.
    D   forgets the names in a Russian novel.

Which answer is partly true?

3 In Paper 3 of the examination you may have to do an 'expansion' exercise. You will be given key words and, by adding prepositions, articles, etc. and choosing the appropriate form of the verbs, you have to expand them into complete sentences. These sentences usually make a complete letter. Make sure you read the whole letter before you start, to get a good idea of the situation. This will be of particular help with deciding on the tense of the verbs.

Note carefully from the examples in the exercise below what kind of alterations need to be made.

City College
Minster Road
York

15th March

Dear Mr and Mrs Turner,

I write / you / son Paul.

a) I am writing to you about your son Paul.

He be / my German class / six months.

b) He has been in my German class for six months.

His pronunciation and grammar / satisfactory / but reading and writing / not improve.

c) ....

I ask him / do / extra reading / home.

d) ....

I wonder / you can encourage / spend half an hour / day / read / German newspaper / magazine.

e) ....

Short novels / graded readers / also available / school library.

f) ....

Thank you / help / this matter.

g) ....

Yours sincerely,

C. Shuttleworth

Section B

1 MINUTE

1 Here is an extract from *Teaching Reading Skills in a Foreign Language* by Christine Nuttall. It is taken from Unit 12 of the book. Skim through the text and decide on the most suitable title for the unit.
  a) Reading in a Foreign Language
  b) Reading Skills
  c) An Intensive Reading Programme
  d) An Extensive Reading Programme

Many of us teach students who are trapped in the vicious circle shown in Figure 25.

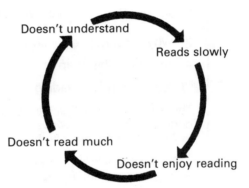

Fig. 25   The vicious circle of the weak reader

It doesn't matter where you enter the circle, because any of the factors that make it up will produce any of the others. A slow reader is seldom able to develop much interest in what he reads, let alone enjoyment. Since he gets no pleasure from it, he reads as little as possible. Deprived of practice, he continues to find it difficult to understand what he reads, so his reading rate does not increase. He remains a slow reader: and so on.

Somehow or other we must help him to get out of this cycle of frustration and enter instead the cycle of growth represented in Figure 26.

As we have seen in earlier chapters, speed, enjoyment and comprehension are closely linked with one another and with the amount of practice a reader gets. Any of the factors could provide the key that will get us out of the vicious circle and into the virtuous one; but the most hopeful, I think, is *enjoyment*, closely followed by *quantity*.

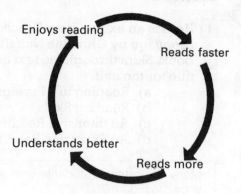

Fig. 26 The virtuous circle of the good reader

2 Why encourage extensive reading?

At the heart of this chapter is the slogan

We learn to read by reading.

This is so unoriginal that I do not know who said it first; and it is perfectly accurate. However, we learn something else by reading too, and this provides another useful slogan:

> The best way to improve your knowledge of a foreign language is to go and live among its speakers. The next best way is to read extensively in it.

2 This text is similar to the text in Section A (pages 24–5). Read the following statements and decide which **one** is correct.

Both Frank Smith and Christine Nuttall claim that
- a) a good reader is someone who enjoys what he/she reads.
- b) a good reader enjoys reading long novels.
- c) the more you read, the more you enjoy reading.
- d) if you enjoy what you read, you are more likely to become a good reader.

3 There are differences between the two texts, however. Read the following statements and decide which **one** is correct.

- a) The authors agree that enjoyment is an important part of reading. However, only Christine Nuttall claims that experience will help you to read faster.
- b) Both authors say that it is important to enjoy reading, but only Frank Smith recommends Russian novels.
- c) Although both authors recommend extensive reading, Frank Smith warns us that we might not be able to remember everything we've read.
- d) While both authors agree that students must be encouraged to read extensively, Frank Smith points out that there is a danger of getting bored or anxious.

4 Look at the four answers to question 3 again. They contain examples of sentences with:

but   however   although   while

Use one of them in each of the spaces in the following exercise. It would help to look back at the linking words exercise in Unit 1, page 5.

- a) Many people are trapped in a vicious circle where lack of understanding leads to lack of enjoyment when reading, and then lack of any reading at all. .... , it is possible to break out of this circle with a little effort.
- b) A relaxed approach to reading will help most people to enjoy it, ... attempts to memorize the characters and events of a story will not.
- c) .... reading in a foreign language will greatly improve your knowledge, it's even better if you can go and live there.
- d) .... practice at reading fast is helpful to a reader trying to break out of the circle, the most important key to successful reading is enjoyment.

5 Exam Practice

In this exercise, choose the word or phrase which best completes each sentence. Remember to look carefully at the grammatical construction of the sentence before making your choice.

1. I wouldn't want to read that sort of book .... attractive the cover might seem.
   A nevertheless B however   C yet   D if

2. The title of the book seemed .... to her.
   A known   B common   C familiar   D personal

3. She isn't put .... by words she doesn't understand.
   A away   B down   C up   D off

4. Have you a rough .... of your reading speed?
   A hope   B imagination   C thought   D idea

5. You can take as many books as you want .... they're back on Monday.
   A ensuring   B expecting   C providing   D supposing

6. No wonder he was a slow reader. He was always .... words in his dictionary!
   A looking to   B looking up   C looking at   D looking for

7   She doesn't read much, and ....
    A nor her brother   B neither her brother
    C nor does her brother   D her brother too

8   When I saw his written English I .... he did much more reading.
    A suggested   B advised   C told   D argued

9   Is this book .... for intermediate students of English?
    A reliable   B suitable   C fashionable   D favourable

10 She was so .... not to be late for the exam that she arrived nearly two hours early.
    A anxious   B excited   C worried   D thoughtful

STUDY HINTS

Look at the last two sentences of the text again:

> The best way to improve your knowledge of a foreign language is to go and live among its speakers. The next best way is to read extensively in it.

You may not have the opportunity to visit an English-speaking country, but there should be no reason why you cannot read extensively in English.

Here are some suggestions:

- Look at an English-language newspaper once a week. If they are not available in your area, ask your newsagent to give you details of subscriptions. You could try the *Guardian Weekly* or *Time Magazine*.

- Read one short novel a month. Your school library, local library or the British Council will be happy to help you. You might like to begin with graded readers until your reading skills improve and you grow in confidence.
    There is also plenty of cartoon material available in English, e.g. *Asterix*, *Tintin* and *Superman*.

- Always try to get an overall understanding of a text first and do not worry about new words. Then try to work out their meaning from the context. Find out or check the meaning in a good English-English dictionary and remember that every time you look up a word you will be practising your reading skills in English. You will quickly learn that an English dictionary contains a lot of useful information and more accurate meanings than the small bilingual dictionary you carry in your pocket.

Section C

 30 SECONDS

1 Here is an extract from *Use Your Head*, by Tony Buzan. Read it quickly and decide if it is written for

a) opticians and oculists.
b) teachers and students.
c) people with poor eyesight.
d) psychologists.

Discuss your choice with a partner.

A

Fig 10 **Assumed reading eye movement as shown by people with no knowledge of eye movements. Each line is thought to be covered in less than one second.**

Relating all this to reading, it is obvious that if the eyes are going to take in words, and if the words are still, the eyes will have to pause on each word before moving on. Rather than moving in smooth lines as shown in fig 10, the eyes in fact move in a series of stops and quick jumps.

B

Fig 11 **Diagram representing the stop-and-start movement of the eyes during the reading process.**

The jumps themselves are so quick as to take almost no time, but the fixations can take anywhere from ¼ to 1½ seconds. A person who normally reads one word at a time – and who skips back over words and letters is forced, by the simple mathematics of his eye movements, into reading speeds which are often well below 100 wpm, and which mean that he will not be able to understand much of what he reads, nor be able to read much.

C

Fig 12 **Diagram showing poor reading habits of slow reader: one word read at a time, with unconscious back-skipping, visual wandering, and conscious regressions.**

It might seem at first glance that the slow reader is doomed, but the problem can be solved, and in more than one way.

Speeding up

1 Skipping back over words can be eliminated, as 90 per cent of back-skipping and regression is based on apprehension and is unnecessary for understanding. The 10 per cent of words that do need to be reconsidered can be noted in Mind Map form as outlined in Chapters 7 and 8 or can be intelligently guessed, marked and looked up later.

2 The time for each fixation can be reduced to approach the ¼ second minimum – the reader need not fear that this is too short a time, for his eye is able to register as many as five words in one one-hundredth of a second.

3 The size of the fixation can be expanded to take in as many as three to five words at a time.

D

Fig 13 **Diagram showing eye movements of a better and more efficient reader. More words are taken in at each fixation, and back-skipping, regression and visual wandering are reduced.**

This solution might at first seem impossible if it is true that the mind deals with one word at a time. In fact it can equally well fixate in *groups* of words, which is better in nearly all ways: When we read a sentence we do not read it for the individual meaning of each word, but for the meaning of the phrases in which the words are contained.

Reading for example, the cat sat on the road is more difficult than reading the cat sat on the road.

The slower reader has to do more mental work than the faster, smoother reader because he has to add the meaning of each word to the meaning of each following word. In the above example this amounts to five or six additions. The more efficient reader, absorbing in meaningful units, has only one simple addition.

ADVANTAGES OF FASTER READING

An advantage for the faster reader is that his eyes will be doing less physical work on each page. Rather than having as many as 500 fixations tightly focused per page as does the slow reader, he will have as few as 100 fixations per page, each one of which is less muscularly fatiguing.

2 Here are the missing diagrams. Match each of them to one of the four parts – A, B, C or D.

1
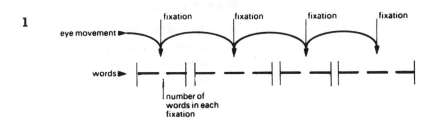

2
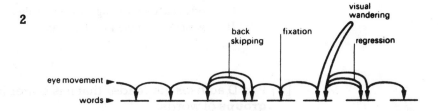

3
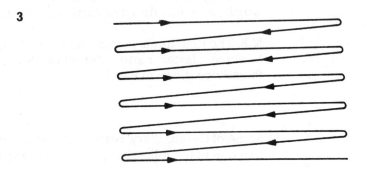

4
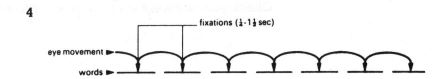

3 Which of the above best represents the way **you** read
  a) a text in your own language?
  b) a text in English?

4 Exam Practice

Now try to answer these multiple choice questions.

1. Fast readers

    A think of each sentence as a group of words.
    B do not have any fixations to slow them down.
    C do not have as many fixations as slow readers.
    D are no good at adding up.

2. Slow readers

    A never understand what they read.
    B get tired sooner than fast readers.
    C often have something wrong with their eye muscles.
    D waste 90% of their reading time.

5

Part D advises the reader that it is better if the mind fixates on **groups** of words.

With a partner, look at the last paragraph of the text (An advantage for ...) and try to divide it into meaningful groups of words, like this: An advantage/for the faster reader/ ...

N.B. The time limits in this book are designed to help you become a faster, more efficient reader. Try to put into practice the advice given in Part D.

6

Some of the auxiliary verbs have been left out of the text below. Use one of the following in each of the spaces:

   can   need   might   has to   have to   is able to   be able to

Check your answers with a partner and then look back at the text.

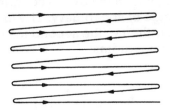

Fig 10 **Assumed reading eye movement as shown by people with no knowledge of eye movements. Each line is thought to be covered in less than one second.**

Relating all this to reading, it is obvious that if the eyes are going to take in words, and if the words are still, the eyes will (1) ..... pause on each word before moving on. Rather than moving in smooth lines as shown in fig 10, the eyes in fact move in a series of stops and quick jumps.

Fig 11 **Diagram representing the stop-and-start movement of the eyes during the reading process.**

The jumps themselves are so quick as to take almost no time, but the fixations (2) ..... take anywhere from ¼ to 1½ seconds. A person who normally reads one word at a time – and who skips back over words and letters is forced, by the simple mathematics of his eye movements, into reading speeds which are often well below 100 wpm, and which mean that he will not (3) ..... understand much of what he reads, nor (4) ..... read much.

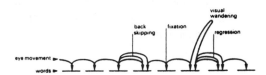

Fig 12 **Diagram showing poor reading habits of slow reader: one word read at a time, with unconscious back-skipping, visual wandering, and conscious regressions.**

It (5) ..... seem at first glance that the slow reader is doomed, but the problem can be solved, and in more than one way.

Speeding up

1 Skipping back over words (6) ..... be eliminated, as 90 per cent of back-skipping and regression is based on apprehension and is unnecessary for understanding. The 10 per cent of words that do (7) ..... to be reconsidered (8) ..... be noted in Mind Map form as outlined in Chapters 7 and 8 or can be intelligently guessed, marked and looked up later.

2 The time for each fixation (9) ..... be reduced to approach the ¼ second minimum – the reader (10) ..... not fear that this is too short a time, for his eye (11) ..... register as many as five words in one one-hundredth of a second.

3 The size of the fixation (12) ..... be expanded to take in as many as three to five words at a time.

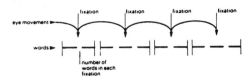

Fig 13 **Diagram showing eye movements of a better and more efficient reader. More words are taken in at each fixation, and back-skipping, regression and visual wandering are reduced.**

This solution (13) ..... at first seem impossible if it is true that the mind deals with one word at a time. In fact it (14) ..... equally well fixate in *groups* of words, which is better in nearly all ways: When we read a sentence we do not read it for the individual meaning of each word, but for the meaning of the phrases in which the words are contained.

Reading for example, the   cat   sat   on
                          the   road   is more difficult than reading
the cat sat   on the road.

The slower reader has to do more mental work than the faster, smoother reader because he (15) ..... add the meaning of each word to the meaning of each following word. In the above example this amounts to five or six additions. The more efficient reader, absorbing in meaningful units, has only one simple addition.

ADVANTAGES OF FASTER READING

An advantage for the faster reader is that his eyes will be doing less physical work on each page. Rather than having as many as 500 fixations tightly focused per page as does the slow reader, he will have as few as 100 fixations per page, each one of which is less muscularly fatiguing.

7 In Paper 3 of the examination, you may have to complete an exercise which tests your range of vocabulary. The first part usually focuses on a particular theme; the second tests your knowledge of phrasal verbs and idioms.

Exam Practice

A Complete the following sentences with **one** word related to the world of **books and literature.** *The first one has been done for you.*

1 A book written by someone about their own life is called an autobiography.
2 The young writer had great difficulty in getting his first book p............................ .
3 ... but it went on to become a highly successful best s............................ .
4 I must go to the library today – this book is already several days o............................ and I'll have to pay a fine.
5 I've got so many books now that I'll have to buy a new b............................ to put them in.

B Complete the following sentences with a phrase made from **look**. *The first one has been done for you.*

1 I'm looking for a book on efficient learning strategies. Do you know where I could get one please?
2 Can I borrow your dictionary please? I need to .... a new word.
3 .... for this season's new titles in your bookshops now!
4 He's really .... to the antique book fair next week – old books have been a passion with him for several years now.
5 Could you just .... this report for me to check that I've included all the important points?

Unit 4　Food

Section A

1 Look at the text and decide if it comes from

　　　a) a playscript.
　　　b) a restaurant guide.
　　　c) a novel.

Discuss your choice with a partner.

Thoughtfully, Kate cut up Hugo's steak and spread each piece with a dab of mustard, then started to turn over her own spinach with her fork, as though inspecting it. Hugo watched her, and then said (for many things that Kate did were little performances, requiring applause, inquiry or comment), 'What are you looking for?'

'Ladybirds,' said Kate.

'Why?'

'Once I had lunch here and ate a ladybird without noticing it.'

'If you didn't notice it, how did you know what it was?'

'Because there was another one, in the spinach. So I thought back, and realized what the crunchy thing was that I'd just eaten. Anyway, I'd kind of half seen it out of the corner of my eye.' Satisfied with her investigation she looped up a mouthful, and ate it. 'It was during that ladybird plague year,' she said, 'do you remember? They were all over the place, swarming on beaches, biting old ladies on the tops of buses. How's your steak?'

'It's fine. But the courgettes taste of chlorine.'

Kate leaned over, helped herself to one, ate it.

'Yes, so they do. Funny, isn't it? I wonder why I go on coming here, it's a terrible restaurant. Loyalty, I suppose.'

'Did you send the spinach back?'

'No, of course not. Women never send things back in restaurants, didn't you know?'

And she smiled at him her wide, infuriating double-edged smile, her smile full of duplicity.

38 FOOD

6 MINUTES

2 Exam Practice

Look at the text again and answer these multiple choice questions.

1. Kate and Hugo are

   A   a father and young child.
   B   an employer and employee.
   C   close friends.
   D   a mother and young child.

2. Kate has eaten in the restaurant

   A   never before.
   B   once before.
   C   several times before.
   D   twice before.

3. Kate didn't want to eat the ladybird because

   A   she's a vegetarian.
   B   it carries the plague.
   C   she's on a diet.
   D   it's an insect.

Look at these two distractors taken from the questions above.

2B   once before
3B   it carries the plague

What do they have in common?

3 Complete the chart. You will find some of the words in the text. The first one has been done for you.

Noun	Verb	Adjective	Adverb
inspection	inspect	————	————
	think		
realization reality			
crunch			
		tasteful tasty	

4 **Exam Practice**

*Fill each of the numbered blanks in this part of the text you have just read. Use only **one** word in each space. Discuss your answers with a partner before looking back at the text.*

Thoughtfully, Kate cut (1) .... Hugo's steak and spread each piece (2) .... a dab of mustard, then started (3) .... turn (4) .... her own spinach (5) .... her fork, as though inspecting it. Hugo watched her, and then said ((6) .... many things that Kate did were little performances, requiring applause, inquiry or comment), 'What are you looking (7) .... ?'

'Ladybirds,' said Kate.

5 Here is another vocabulary exercise like the one you met in Unit 3, page 36.

A   *Fill each gap with **one** word related to the subject of **food**.*

1)   The meat was so ..t............................ I was unable to chew it properly.
2)   I ate a lot of rich food for dinner and it kept me awake the whole night with .i............................. .
3)   I prefer .so........................... food to sweet food.
4)   Can I have a .b............................. of your apple please?
5)   I got a piece of biscuit stuck in my throat and I couldn't .s............................. it.

B   *Fill each gap with a phrase made from **go**.*

1)   That fish has definitely .... ; it smells disgusting.
2)   The price of good wine keeps on .... It's getting really expensive.
3)   The holiday was terrible; we both .... with food poisoning.
4)   I'm getting fat – I need to .... a diet.
5)   She's such a good cook. She should .... for the local competition.

Section B

5 SECONDS

1 Where would you find this text?

Paper Napkins

DEAR MISS MANNERS:
Why can't I use paper napkins – the heavy kind – at a dinner party? They look all right, do the job, and it's more practical to be able to throw them away instead of cleaning them, but some people are fussy about them.

GENTLE READER:
The identical claims were made, a few years ago, for paper underpants. How come you don't wear them?

---

2 Read the text again and answer the following questions.

a) Who is Miss Manners, do you think?
b) What is a napkin? Give evidence from the text to support your answer.
c) What type of napkin does Miss Manners use, and why?

3 Now look at this question about spaghetti and discuss with a partner how you would reply to it.

Spaghetti

DEAR MISS MANNERS:
How do you eat spaghetti with a spoon?

---

4 Compare your ideas with Miss Manners' reply:

GENTLE READER:
Bite your tongue. This is not an eating instruction, but an old-fashioned reprimand to anyone who would even entertain such an outrageous idea as eating spaghetti with a spoon.

Actually, there simply is no easy, foolproof way to eat spaghetti, and that is just as well when you think of how gloriously fat we would all be if there were. The inevitable slippage of spaghetti from the fork back onto the plate is Nature's way of controlling human piggishness. A fork is the only utensil that may be used to eat spaghetti while anyone is looking. It must make do with whatever cooperation it may muster from the plate and the teeth. The fork is planted on the plate, and the spaghetti is then twirled around the tines of the fork. If you can manage to use the grated Parmesan cheese to add grit to the mixture for better control, so much the better. The twirled forkful is then presented to the mouth. If this were an ideal world, all the spaghetti strands would begin and end in the same place, so that the mouth could receive the entire forkful at once. However, we have all learned that compromises must often be made, and the fact is that one will often find a few long strands hanging down outside of the mouth.

As you may not spit these parts back onto the plate, what are you to do with them? Well, for heaven's sake. Why do you think God taught you to inhale?

5 Which of these pictures best represents Miss Manners' advice?

6 Here are four words from the text. Match them to the pictures.

i. twirl (v.)
ii. piggishness (n.)
iii. inhale (v.)
iv. tines (n.)

 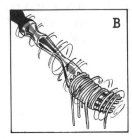 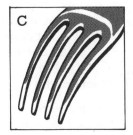 

7 Look at the text again and replace the words above with your own words (so that the meaning stays the same).

e.g. ... and the spaghetti is then twirled around the ⟦tines⟧ of the fork.
⟦ends⟧

Section C

5 SECONDS

1 Where would you find this text?

2 Scan the text to find out how much the following orders would cost.

i. medium ham and pineapple
ii. large Vegi
iii. large pepperoni and mushroom with extra cheese and onions
iv. two medium Hawaiians and one Coke
v. a medium Full House, a large Vegi with extra anchovies and three Cokes
(all delivered in 25 minutes)

3 **Exam Practice**

A wants a pizza and is telephoning Domino's.
Complete the dialogue.

A: Hello

B: Domino's Pizza. Can I help you?

A: Yes, I'd like two ham and mushroom pizzas, please.

B: What .... ?

A: Er, medium.

B: Would .... ?

A: Er, yes, one with extra anchovies.

B: So, that's two medium ham and mushroom, one with anchovies. Anything .... ?

A: No, thanks.

B: Can .... ?

A: 40 Elms Road.

B: Is .... ?

A: No, it's near the bus station, not the railway station.

B: Right. We'll ....

A: OK. Bye.

4 Here is a role-play to do with a partner. Before starting, prepare what you want to say.

Student A: You are telephoning the pizza delivery service with a complicated order. In the middle of the order, you suddenly change your mind. Don't forget to check the prices.

Student B: You take the orders at Domino's Pizza. The phone rings. Make sure you note down exactly what the customer wants and don't forget to check his/her address and telephone number. Remember to be polite.

Now swap roles.

5 **Exam Practice**

Finish each of the following sentences in such a way that it means exactly the same as the sentence printed before it. The first one has been done for you.

a) My lunch is delivered to the office at one o'clock every day.

   I have *my lunch delivered to the office at one o'clock every day.*

b) Eating too much sugar is bad for your teeth.

   It's ....

c) A good meal in London will cost you at least £15.

   You will ....

d) Peter asked Robert if he was going out for dinner.

   'Robert, ...

e)   You won't get a table unless you book well in advance.

   If ……………………………………………………………………………………

f)   It's part of a restaurant manager's job to hire and fire staff.

   A restaurant manager is responsible …………………………………………

g)   David studied for four years and then qualified as a chef.

   After …………………………………………………………………………………

h)   Mary promised to return the casserole dish by Friday.

   'I ……………………………………………………………………………………

i)   'Will I ever own my own restaurant?' Max said to himself.

   Max wondered ……………………………………………………………………

j)   Weights are measured on kitchen scales.

   Kitchen scales are ………………………………………………………………

6 *In this exercise, choose the word or phrase which best completes each sentence.*

1   This curry is hot, but that one's ………… hotter!
   A   more   B   less   C   even   D   also

2   Did you remember ………… the garlic?
   A   buy   B   having bought
   C   to buy   D   have bought

3   They looked ………… they hadn't eaten for days.
   A   as if   B   that   C   so as   D   like that

4   After trying for several days, she ………… to make a perfect souffle.
   A   succeeded   B   managed   C   raised   D   achieved

5   ………… you do, don't open the oven door!
   A   However   B   Nevertheless C   Whatever   D   Whenever

6   We've had a different type of pasta every day ………… we arrived in Italy three weeks ago!
   A   that   B   since   C   because   D   for

7   Try some jelly. It won't ………… you!
   A   damage   B   hurt   C   injure   D   finish

8   I don't like plain chocolate much; it's got such a ………… taste.
   A   sour   B   bad   C   bitter   D   heavy

9 I'll start cooking as soon as I .... the vegetables.
   A have prepared   B will have prepared
   C had prepared   D having prepared

10 It was very .... of her to do the washing-up after the dinner party.
    A grateful   B beautiful   C hopeful   D thoughtful

STUDY HINTS

Here is a suggestion. Try it for a while but if you find it doesn't suit your learning style, don't worry. There are more suggestions in the units that follow.

Keep a small notebook in your pocket at all times. Write down new vocabulary and grammar points with an example of how to use them. Whenever you have a spare moment (e.g. on the bus, in the bathroom, while you're having a cigarette) look at the things you have written this week and one or two things from earlier weeks.

It can help to include pictures and diagrams and use different coloured pens.

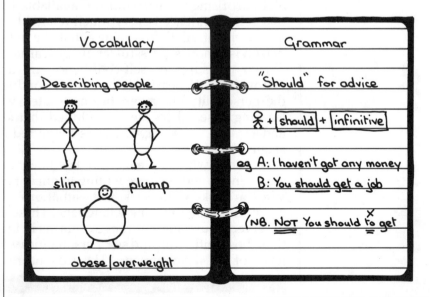

Unit 5 Language

Section A

30 SECONDS

1 Look at the following text and decide where it might come from.

> **Self-Confidence**
>
> Not surprisingly, nearly all the available literature suggests that self-confidence is very much related to second language development. All things being equal, the self-confident, secure person is a more successful language learner.
>
> Two measures of self-confidence are anxiety level and extroversion. In nearly all the studies conducted to determine the personality characteristics associated with successful L_2 learning, researchers have concluded that *lower anxiety levels* and a *tendency to be outgoing* were connected with successful L_2 acquisition.
>
> Learners who are eager to try new and unpredictable experiences, and who are willing to guess before knowing for sure, are likely to seek out situations that require real communication in the new language. These people have been observed to use a larger range of forms in the target language than those with 'wait and see' personalities who are at the same level of L_2 development. The adventuresome have been

observed to find language learning relatively painless and to learn fairly quickly.

The studies that led to these conclusions were described in the previous chapter in the section on the filter. They do not show precisely how self-confidence and language learning relate, but they do demonstrate the existence of the relationship. We suggest that self-confident people have the advantage of not fearing rejection as much as those with high anxiety levels and are therefore more likely to put themselves in learning situations and to do so repeatedly. They are thrown into less personal turmoil when they make mistakes than those who are more self-conscious. This probably enhances subconscious language learning because they are more able to take in and process what they hear at any given moment.

4 MINUTES

2 Exam Practice

Read the text again and answer the following multiple choice questions.

1 The writer claims that

   A self-confident people are good at languages.
   B people who are good at languages are self-confident.
   C if you learn a foreign language you also learn self-confidence.
   D self-confidence helps you to learn languages.

2 Self-confident people

   A are louder than other language learners.
   B speak more than other language learners.
   C make more mistakes than other language learners.
   D spend more time studying than other language learners.

3 Look at the text again and find one word which means the same as:

   a) feeling of nervousness (n.)
   b) impossible to know about in advance (adj.)
   c) being afraid of (v.)
   d) state of confusion and uncertainty (n.)
   e) improves the quality of (v.)

4 Without looking back at the text, choose one word to fill each gap in the following sentences.

a) Learners .... are eager to try new and unpredictable experiences, and .... are willing to guess before knowing for sure, are likely to seek out situations .... require real communication in the new language.

b) The studies .... led to these conclusions were described in the previous chapter.

c) They are thrown into less personal turmoil than those .... are more self-conscious.

Now look back at the text to check your answers.

5 In one of these sentences, the relative pronoun is not necessary. Can you say which one it is, and why?

a) Students ...who........ are self-confident will generally learn much faster than those ....who........ are not.

b) Anxiety, ...which...... tends to block the learning process, is less likely to occur if the student is not worried about making mistakes.

c) A technique ....that........ I have always found useful is to concentrate on getting my message across effectively rather than worry about accuracy.

6 Exam Practice

In this exercise, choose the word or phrase which best completes each sentence.

1   I went home again to .... my dictionary.
      A   take   B   bring   C   gather   D   fetch

2   I found it very difficult to .... myself understood when I went to China.
      A   be   B   make   C   find   D   have

3   He .... speaking English unless he really has to.
      A   avoids   B   prevents   C   hinders   D   refuses

4   They can come to class tomorrow .... they have paid.
      A   so long   B   in case   C   unless   D   provided

5   He tries very hard, but is .... of understanding English spoken outside the classroom.
      A   incapable   B   terrible   C   unable   D   impossible

6 I make a .... of all new vocabulary because I need to see it written down before I can remember it.
   A notebook   B notice   C description   D list

7 They said they were .... for the free conversation lessons.
   A grateful   B thoughtful   C pleased   D delighted

8 She had a great .... of languages.
   A desire   B love   C like   D enthusiasm

9 They're quite happy to use their English .... the many little mistakes they make.
   A even though B in spite of C in addition to D however

10 Studying languages .... a lot of hard work.
   A asks   B offers   C concerns   D involves

Section B

1 The next text is taken from *Linguistics in Language Teaching* by D. A. Wilkins, a book for language teachers.
Here is the title of a chapter.

Error and the mother-tongue

What do you think the chapter will be about? Make a list of possibilities and then discuss your ideas with a partner.

LANGUAGE

1 MINUTE

Now read the text to see if you were right.

7.1 The evidence of mother-tongue interference

If we were to wander into a classroom where pupils were learning a foreign language and if we listened to them speaking that language or observed their attempts to write it, we should notice before long that the same mistakes of pronunciation, spelling, grammar and vocabulary tended to recur in the language of different individuals. In time, too, we should probably be able to identify the mother-tongue of the pupils even if not a word of it had been spoken in the classroom.[1] We should be able to do this solely on the basis of the recurring mistakes that we had noticed. Our ability to recognize the provenance of somebody who speaks our language with an accent, for example, is used by entertainers the world over. Comedians can be sure of raising an easy laugh with a portrayal of the German speaking English, the Englishman speaking French or the American speaking Spanish.

If, therefore, we look at the speech and writing of the foreign language learner, there is little reason to doubt that we will find many mistakes which can be traced back to the mother-tongue. The comedian probably gets most, though not all, of his effects by imitating the foreigner's pronunciation, but in fact evidence of the mother-tongue is found on a far wider scale than this, even if it is not always recognized. It might be useful to begin this discussion by demonstrating the extent to which a learner uses features of his native language in his attempts to speak and write in the foreign language. If we imagine the efforts of a learner to produce the English sentence:

His wife wants to pay her grandfather a visit in the old people's home

we should be able to see some of the substitutions from the mother-tongue that are made by different learners and that cause errors.

[1] Provided, of course, the mother-tongue was not a language that was utterly strange to us.

2 Here are three summaries of the first paragraph. Which is best, and why?

a) Students make the same types of mistake, and we can notice these in the classroom. Comedians often pretend to be foreigners to make people laugh.

b) Making mistakes in a foreign language is funny.

c) Students from the same country tend to make the same mistakes. From this, it is possible to work out the mother-tongue of a student even if we don't know where he/she is from. Comedians often use this fact to make people laugh.

3 Exam Practice

Read the second paragraph and answer this multiple choice question.

The writer claims that

- A   errors are caused by the mother-tongue.
- B   errors in pronunciation are caused by the mother-tongue.
- C   the mother-tongue causes many types of error.
- D   the mother-tongue causes errors which make people laugh.

4 Do the following expansion exercise to help you write a summary of the second paragraph.

Many mistakes/make/learner/cause/mother-tongue interference.
Although comedians/jokes/pronunciation/mother-tongue interference/recognize/other areas.
A learner/mistakes/try/translate/mother-tongue.

5 Without looking back at the text, fill the gaps in the following sentences with the appropriate form of the verb in brackets. The first one has been done for you.

If we (be) (1) ...**were**...... to wander into a classroom where pupils (learn) (2) .... a foreign language and if we (listen) (3) .... to them speaking that language or (observe) (4) .... their attempts to write it, we (notice) (5) .... before long that the same mistakes of pronunciation, spelling, grammar and vocabulary (tend) (6) .... to recur in the language of different individuals.

6 Now do the same with the following sentences.

If, therefore, we (look) (1) ...**look**....... at the speech and writing of the foreign language learner, there (be) (2) .... little reason to doubt that we (find) (3) .... many mistakes which can be traced back to the mother-tongue. The comedian probably (get) (4) .... most, though not all, of his effects by imitating the foreigner's pronunciation, but in fact evidence of the mother-tongue (find) (5) .... on a far wider scale than this, even if it (be) (6) .... not always recognized.

Compare your answers with a partner's and then check with the text.

7 Both paragraphs begin with 'If', but how are they different? Discuss your ideas first with your partner and then with your teacher.

STUDY HINTS

Monolingual classes

It will help you if you become aware of grammatical, phonological or lexical errors that you make as a result of mother-tongue interference. Discuss this type of error with the rest of the class or group, and then with your teacher. Make a list and try to work through it systematically.

Multilingual classes

Always pair up with a student with a different mother-tongue when checking work (spoken or written).
You could make a list of the major errors caused by your own mother-tongue and then swap your list with someone else in the class. You could then monitor each other's progress.

Section C

1 Here is an extract from *Discover English*, by Rod Bolitho and Brian Tomlinson, a book that provides exercises on problem areas in English. It is aimed at advanced learners and teachers of English. Complete the exercises on your own or with a partner.

a) Look at this statement and decide if you agree.

> 'English is a stupid language. It is illogical and irregular and it follows no rules.'

Give examples of irregularities and illogicalities in English.

Here is part of the suggested response to the statement.

> A language cannot be said to be stupid because it is not completely regular and is not completely controlled by rules. No living language is completely regular and rule bound because living languages are organic and are constantly being changed by their users.
> It is common for learners of a language to think that their own language is logical and regular whereas the one they are learning is stupidly irregular. This is usually because they very seldom examine their own language whereas they are frequently called upon to examine the language they are learning. They also find their own language easy to use and assume that this is because it is logical and regular.

Did you think of these points?

b) Look at the columns from top to bottom and note down any rules you can see.

1	2	3	4
swimming	It's hot, isn't it?	He bought it.	Have you got any money?
dining	She's fat, isn't she?	She grew it.	
sinned	You didn't come, did you?	He brought it.	Have you got some money?
lined	I've won, haven't I?	I showed them.	
hatred	She'll come, won't she?	He wanted it.	Give me some books.
baited	He wasn't happy, was he?	I cleaned it.	Give me any books.
getting	The bus is late, isn't it?	I blamed them. He cheated them.	We haven't got any more.
greeting	Mary had finished, hadn't she?	I went there. He sold it.	We haven't got some more.

54 LANGUAGE

2 Think about your own language.

Can you give examples of how the grammar rules have changed in the last 50 years?

Can you give examples of illogicalities and irregularities?

3 Look at the text again and find words or expressions that mean the same as:

    a) living/growing (adj.)
    b) while/but (conj.)
    c) not ... often (adv.)
    d) often (adv.)
    e) suppose (v.)

4 Here are five more statements about English.
Do you agree with them?
Discuss your ideas with a partner.

a) 'You don't need a teacher to learn a foreign language. All you need is a grammar book and a dictionary.'

b) '*Some* is only used in positive statements whereas *any* is used in negative statements and questions.'

c) 'Countable nouns refer to things which you can count (e.g. *chairs, books, apples*) whereas uncountable nouns refer to things which you cannot count (e.g. *rice, soap, money*).'

d) 'The past tenses always refer to the past – e.g. *He was going to the match.*'

e) '*will* is never used in clauses which begin with *when, after, before* or *as soon as*.'

Match the following suggested responses to the statements above.

i. Tense is not the same as time reference. The past tenses are often used with past time reference but not always (e.g. *I was thinking of going to the match tomorrow; I wondered if you would allow us to miss the meeting; If he came it would be too late*).

ii. *Will* is used in such clauses with the function of expressing *willingness* (e.g. *Let me know when he will do it*). The statement is designed to prevent such errors as, x *I will phone you when he will arrive*, and can be a fairly useful over-simplification if it is made less absolute (e.g. *not often* instead of *never*).

iii.	This statement is demonstrably untrue (e.g. *Have you found some?*; *I'll deal with any questions at the end*). However, at an early stage of language learning it might be a useful over-simplification to make to certain learners providing that the truth is subsequently revealed.
iv.	This statement is confusing as it is obvious that you can count money. It would be more accurate to say that uncountable nouns cannot be preceded by a number (e.g. x *two rices*; x *four monies*). N.B. x = incorrect utterance.
v.	Grammar books and dictionaries are important sources of information about a language. They can teach someone about a language but they cannot teach anyone to use a language as they cannot expose the learner to language in real use and they do not provide any opportunities for practice or production.

5 Here is another word-building exercise.
What two things do you have to remember before you start?
(see Unit 1, page 10)

Exam Practice

Fill each blank with a suitable word formed from the word in capitals.

a) The writer makes the .... that self-confidence is related to second language development.   SUGGEST

b) Psychological .... is important to language learning.   SECURE

c) An .... learner is often a poor learner.   ANXIETY

d) .... to try new experiences can lead the learner into truly communicative situations.   EAGER

e) The studies do not show the precise .... between self-confidence and language learning.   RELATE

f) There is a greater .... that they will put themselves into a learning situation.   LIKELY

56 LANGUAGE

6 *Make all the changes and additions necessary to produce, from the following sets of words and phrases, sentences which together make a complete letter.*
Remember to read right through the letter before you begin, and to check that all the verbs are in the correct form. Note carefully from the example what kind of alterations need to be made.

Dear Sarah,

As you can see / this letter / I still / Turkey.

a) As you can see from this letter I am still in Turkey.

The weather / wonderful / the people / friendly.

b) ....

I not think / ever come back!

c) ....

I start / learn Turkish.

d) ....

I go / classes / twice / week / but / not make much progress.

e) ....

I remember / what / say in class / but outside / forget / immediately.

f) ....

The grammar / okay because / regular.

g) ....

It / vocabulary / I / not remember.

h) ....

I suppose / practice / more confidence / get better.

i) ....

See you soon?

Lots of love,

Ben

Unit 6   Travel

Section A

1 MINUTE

1 Here is an extract from a travel book called *Arabia*, by Jonathan Raban. It is divided into three parts. Read Part A and answer the multiple choice question.

The action takes place in

    a) a workshop.
    b) Kaddouri.
    c) a tax haven.
    d) somewhere else.

> An instructor took me through the warren of workshops. In the language laboratory, students with earphones clamped over their head-dresses were picking up Job English. The textbook they were working from struck me as a shaming example of the indifference that Kaddouri had talked of.
>
>   *'Hello, Mrs Jones. Would you like some coffee?'*
>   *'Yes please, Mrs Smith.'*
>   *'Do you like sugar and milk in your coffee?'*
>   *'I want milk but no sugar please, Mrs Smith.'*
>
> No doubt the author of this cosy sludge is sitting in a tax haven somewhere. I hope he is troubled by the occasional twinge of conscience. He would probably, sadly, be reassured to hear that I watched a class of Yemenis and Qataris poring diligently over every word of his awful dialogue.

58 TRAVEL

1 MINUTE

2 Now read Part B. You may need to amend your answer to question 1 before answering the following multiple choice question.

The action takes place in

    a) a traditional Arab house.
    b) a technical school in an Arabic-speaking country.
    c) Cheltenham.
    d) somewhere else.

A happier hut housed a group of trainee draughtsmen learning to design arches. They were being taught by an enthusiastic Indian who explained that it was important to learn how to make arches in the Arab world; it was part of the tradition. The arches looked fine to me, and the Indian instructor had made up his own course based on a study of Arab architecture. He showed me plans of houses which adapted modern building techniques to the layout of the traditional Arab house with its courtyard, arches, male and female quarters. I said that I wished the writers of English textbooks had half his sensitivity to the needs of the people he was teaching.

'English,' he said, 'is a very important language. The people go to English; English is too important to go to the people.'

I interrupted another group of students who were being shown how to take television sets to pieces. The Qataris among them had all been to London. Where, I asked them, had they been?

They enumerated the places carefully.

'Earls Court. The Cromwell Road. South Kensington. Gloucester Road.'

'Cheltenham,' said an eccentric.

'When you were in England, did you meet English people and make English friends?'

'No. I see my cousins. They are staying in one hotel, I am staying in another.'

'Did you enjoy being in London?'

'I like London very much. Very good city. I go to London again in June.'

'But you will not meet Londoners?'

'No. Is very difficult.'

'What do you like most about London?'

'The pubs.'

'The girls.'

'The Museum of Science and Natural History.'

When reading any text, remember that you must not reach conclusions about it too quickly.

3 Here are some words from Part A.
Decide whether they carry a positive/complimentary meaning or a negative/pejorative meaning and complete the table below.

*shaming   cosy   sludge   twinge
indifference   diligently   awful*

awful

4 **Exam Practice**

Answer the following multiple choice question, which relates to Part A of the text.

The writer feels that

A   the students are wasting their time.
B   Kaddouri doesn't care about his students.
C   the author of the textbook is unhappy.
D   the students should have better textbooks to learn from.

5 What is the author's main criticism of the dialogue in Part A? (You will find the answer to this question in Part B.)

6 Which of the following dialogues would the writer prefer, and why?

a) Mohammed: Hello Ahmed. Would you like some coffee?
Ahmed: Yes please, Mohammed.
Mohammed: Would you like some milk?
Ahmed: Yes please.
Mohammed: Would you like some sugar?
Ahmed: Yes please.

b) Mohammed: Hello Ahmed.
Ahmed: Hi! How are things?
Mohammed: Okay. Do you want a coffee?
Ahmed: Er, yeah okay.
Mohammed: Sugar and milk?
Ahmed: Just milk, thanks.

c) Mohammed: Ahmed?
Ahmed: Yes?
Mohammed: Can I borrow your calculator a minute?
Ahmed: Er ... yeah. Here you are.
Mohammed: Thanks.

7 Look at dialogues (a) and (b) above.
How are they different?
Which do **you** prefer, and why?

8 **Exam Practice**

Part B of the text contains a dialogue between the writer and a group of students. Correct/amend the responses and complete the following dialogue.

Writer: Where did you go when you were in England?

Student: ....

Writer: Did you meet English people and make English friends?

Student: ....

Writer: Did you enjoy being in London?

Student: ....

Writer: But you will not meet Londoners?

Student: ....

Writer: What do you like most about London?

Student: ....

9 *Fill each of the numbered blanks in the following passage taken from Part A of the text. Use **one preposition** in each space.*

An instructor took me (1) .... the warren (2) .... workshops. (3) .... the language laboratory, students (4) .... earphones clamped (5) .... their head-dresses were picking (6) .... Job English. The textbook they were working (7) .... struck me as a shaming example

(8) .... the indifference that Kaddouri had talked
(9) ....

Check your answers with a partner and then check with Part A of the text.

10 *Finish each of the following sentences in such a way that it means exactly the same as the sentence printed before it. The first one has been done for you.*

a) They were sorry they hadn't met her at the station.

They regretted ....*not meeting her at the station.*........................

b) To get the 15% discount, you must book your ticket at least 14 days in advance.

You can only ....

c) It's pointless to have that old car repaired.

That old car is not ....

d) Bob's new motor-bike has a 125cc engine.

Bob has a new motor-bike ....

e) Mary paid £2,000 for her second-hand car; it was really cheap!

Mary's second-hand car ....

f) 'I'm sorry I gave you the wrong departure time,' said the tourist agent.

The tourist agent apologised ....

"DRIVE IT? **DRIVE** IT?! ARE YOU MAD, MAN?"

g) The stable boys feed the horses at 6 a.m. every day.

The horses ....

h) We've run out of petrol.

There ....

i) A policeman showed me the way.

I was ....

j) If you don't finish your schoolwork now, you won't enjoy your trip on Sunday.

Unless ....

Section B

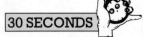

1 Look quickly at this letter and decide if Chris and M. are
   a) business associates.
   b) friends.
   c) father and daughter.
   d) related in another way.

CAIRO

22nd October

Hello Chris,

I arrived Cairo last 17th, this city is caotic, I don't know much about it, but I think it's a very suitable to me, what do you think? I remember you told me you lived in Cairo for a while and I wonder if you're so kind to tell me anything about this city and if you could give to me some advice to improve my live here. I don't know, exactly, how long I'll stay here, but I'll be a few months at least, I want to go on study English, it's obvious I need it, I'm going to start in November in the British Council, what do you thing? Could you tell me anything else? Please, HELP!

I am waiting for you letter. Please don't forget it and do it as soon as you can, I know your time is gold, but, maybe, you could give to me some of your valuable time, can you? Thank you.

Take care and bee a good boy.

4 MINUTES

2 **Exam Practice**

Now answer these multiple choice questions.

1 M. is writing to Chris because

    A she would like to know the city better.
    B she is unhappy in Cairo.
    C she is lonely and misses Chris.
    D she wants to know if she should go to Britain to study English.

2 In her letter, M.

    A implies that she will probably enjoy Cairo.
    B implies that she is on holiday.
    C says that this is her first visit to Cairo.
    D says she is staying in Cairo till November.

3 Look at these two corrected versions of part of M's letter. Decide which one you think is better, and why, and discuss your ideas with a partner.

1 Dear Chris,

I arrived here last week. I don't know much about Cairo, which is a really chaotic city, but I think it's the right place for me. What do you think? As you used to live here, perhaps you could give me some advice on places to go and things to see.

2 Dear Chris,

I arrived in Cairo last week. It is chaotic. I don't know much about it. I think it's the right place for me. What do you think? You used to live here, didn't you? Can you give me any advice on places to go and things to see?

4 Now correct the spelling and grammar in the rest of the letter.

5 Exam Practice

Here is Chris's reply to M.'s letter. Make all the changes and additions necessary to produce, from the following sets of words and phrases, sentences which together make a complete letter. Note carefully from the example what kind of alterations need to be made.

London
Nov. 5th

Dear Mercedes,

I / very surprised / receive your letter.

a) I was very surprised to receive your letter.

I think you / South America!

b) ....

not / Cairo / wonderful city?

c) ....

I call / friend last night / and he / contact you soon.

d) ....

His name / Mohammed / and live / Heliopolis.

e) ....

British Council / good school.

f) ....

I work there / two years.

g) ....

If you arrive / month earlier / you join / First Certificate class.

h) ....

Still, if you decide / stay / you can start / spring.

i) ....

Have fun and write again soon.

Love,

Chris

6 Here are two postcards. They are written by students of English.

Underline any mistakes and discuss them with a partner. Write a corrected version of each postcard.

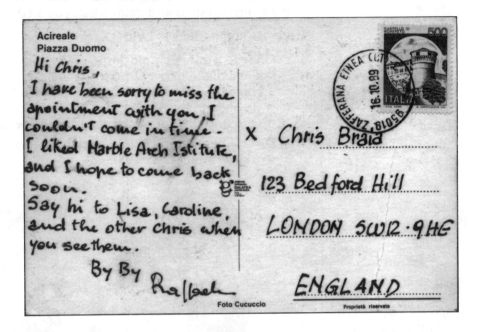

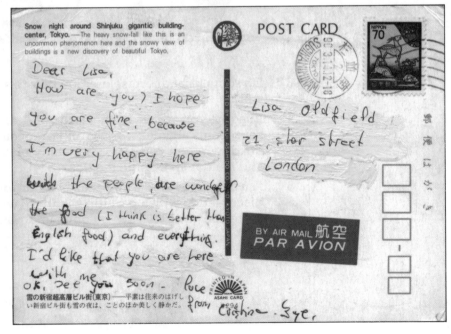

STUDY HINTS

In Unit 5, pages 46–7, we saw that anxiety and stress have a bad effect on language learning. However, what could be more stressful than taking an exam? It is important, therefore, that you are relaxed and calm when you sit down to study.

Here are some ideas to help.

1. Choose a quiet, comfortable place to study in. Going to a special place like a library often has a psychological advantage. When you have finished working, you can walk out and leave the place behind. You will then be free to switch your mind off and enjoy yourself.

2. Discipline yourself to do regular but short amounts of work (30 minutes a day?).

3. Do some light exercise or yoga before sitting down to work.

4. Imagine you are wearing a large and strange hat. The hat represents all your worries and preoccupations during the day. When you go to your study place, take off the hat and hang it up outside the door.

5. Any language items that cause you problems should be discussed a) with a partner/friend; b) with your teacher. Never be afraid to say you don't understand.

TRAVEL 67

Section C

30 SECONDS

1 Skim read this passage and decide if it is

a) a factual description of the countryside.
b) an article from a magazine.
c) a set of directions for drivers.
d) a set of directions for walkers.

Cormorants lay their eggs on cliff tops in the early spring.

ROUTE DIRECTIONS
Allow 3 hours.
Start from the large car park a few hundred yards before Polkerris.

At the beach turn left and go up the path, ignoring a flight of steps on the right. Continue uphill until reaching a quiet road. Turn right here.

Follow the road, keeping straight ahead at Tregaminion Chapel until reaching Menabilly Barton. Follow the track, keeping left at the junction as you pass through the farm that leads down to Polridmouth Cove.

At the wooden stile above the cove, turn right and follow the coast path. On reaching an open field, make directly for the tall beacon tower above Gribbin Head.

From the beacon, follow the coast path along the western side of the headland, keeping left at all junctions.

Where the path reaches the trees above Polkerris, walk along the brow of the wood, ignoring the stiles, until reaching a coast footpath sign. This path leads down a series of inclines to the cove and back to the car park.

2 MINUTES

2 Which of the following best represents the directions given?

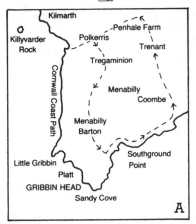

A

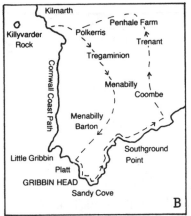

B

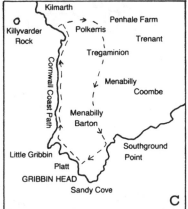

C

3 Here are some words from the text. They are probably new to you. Can you work out their meaning? Decide whether a) or b) is the correct definition.

1) track
   a) like a road, but larger
   b) like a road, but smaller

2) cove
   a) like a river
   b) like a bay, but smaller

3) stile
   a) a type of tree
   b) a type of gate

4) beacon
   a) a strong light or fire
   b) a pile of stones to mark the top of the hill

5) headland
   a) like a valley
   b) like a cliff

6) brow
   a) highest edge
   b) lowest edge

7) inclines
   a) steps
   b) slopes

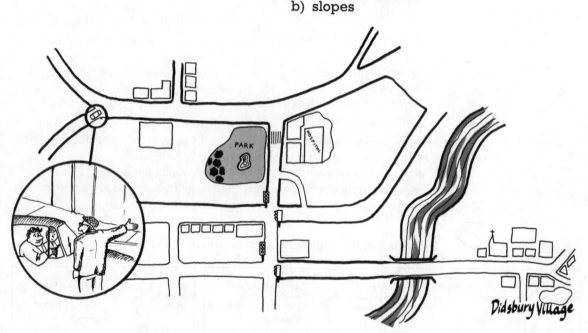

Didsbury Village

4 **Exam Practice**

Look at the map and, using ideas from the passage, complete the dialogue.

A: Excuse me.

B: ....

A: I'm afraid we're a little lost.

B: ....

A: I wonder if you could tell us how to get to Didsbury Village.

B: ....
....

A: Left at the ... ?

B: ....

A: Thank you very much indeed.

B: ....

5

A *In this exercise, fill the gaps with **one** word related to **travel**.*

1. I must remember to **b**................... my tickets to the Bahamas earlier this year. Last year I was too late and had to go to the Canaries instead.
2. When you enter a foreign country you have to go through **c**................... with your luggage before you can leave the airport.
3. It's a good idea to change money into the local **c**................... before you go in case the banks are shut when you arrive.
4. What a lovely fan!
   It's a **s**................... from Japan.
5. The travel agent gave me a lot of **b**................... to help me decide where to go for my holiday.

B *In this exercise, complete the sentences with a phrase made from **take**.*

1. Fasten your seat belts please – the plane is about to ....
2. Help! The hijacker has entered the cockpit and .... the controls!
3. I'm going to .... fishing as my holiday hobby this year. I'm going to Ireland for three weeks of total relaxation.
4. I think I've .... too much this time. I'll never be able to walk the whole length of the Great Wall of China in three weeks.
5. Mary has written at least ten letters to the young waiter she met on holiday. She was very .... him.

6 *In this exercise, choose the word or phrase which best completes each sentence.*

1. The farmer .... me to take the second turning on the left, but I ended up in a field instead of at the B & B place!
   A suggested   B explained   C said   D advised

2. We .... better take lots of things to do indoors – it rains non-stop in Ireland.
   A should   B are   C had   D would

3. We decided to climb up the mountain .... the bad weather.
   A in spite   B despite   C on account   D although

4. When he returned to his hotel room, he discovered he had been ....
   A taken   B thieved   C stolen   D robbed

5. They had a great .... of trouble getting through the customs.
   A lot   B level   C deal   D quantity

6. It was awful. We were just over .... there when a storm broke and we all got soaked.
   A halfway   B some way   C long way   D part way

7. The car .... is two miles from the city centre!
   A park   B parking   C garage   D place

8. Go down the road .... the post office and turn left.
   A as long as   B as far as   C as near as   D as close to

9. I .... indoors yesterday because I got sunburnt.
   A must stay   B ought to stay
   C must have stayed   D had to stay

10. If he left at 3p.m., he ought to .... to my place before dinner tonight.
    A arrive   B reach   C get   D be

Unit 7 Animals

Section A

1 Which of these three animals is a squirrel?

With a partner, make a list of anything you know about these three animals:

- name?
- size?
- colour?
- dangerous?

2 Discuss the set of pictures below with a partner and try to guess what the story that follows is about.

72 ANIMALS

2 MINUTES

Read the story and put the pictures into the correct order.

N.B. There are probably a number of words in this text you don't know. It is above the level of text you will meet in the exam but has been chosen to demonstrate that you do not need to know every word to understand and enjoy a text.

Glancing out of the kitchen window on the Saturday afternoon, I noticed two squirrels at the bottom of the garden. And then I saw the blood. By the time I reached the scene, the grey hooligan was half-way up the nearest tree, leaving his victim in a sorry state: unconscious, blood-stained, and racked by convulsions. I briefly considered putting it out of its misery, but then copped out. The RSPCA would know what to do.

'Are you sure it's an emergency?' asked the emergency service.

'Oh yes, it's on its last legs. Blood everywhere. Pain ... '

'We'll be there in half an hour,' said the capable voice, reassuringly.

I'd placed the squirrel in a plastic bowl and put it in an empty room upstairs. Its mentor arrived in the shape of a huge man with the biggest hands I've ever seen. We trooped upstairs and I opened the door quietly. The animal was now sitting upright but with its head drooping to the floor. There was no movement.

'I think it's gone,' I whispered, and right on cue it opened one baleful eye and then the other.

'I don't think so,' said the large-handed man authoritatively. The squirrel glared up at us fixedly. With the benefit of hindsight, I wonder why I automatically assume losers are always nice.

'Perhaps it's going into a coma,' I said gently.

'I don't think so,' said the ham-fisted one cautiously.

I moved towards it. 'I wouldn't do that, actually,' he said.
'Why?'
These were the last calm words that anyone uttered for some time. The squirrel suddenly appeared to levitate as it powered towards us.
'Look out!' we both yelled as we dived in different directions.
The miraculously arisen squirrel bounced off the door between us, spun round, and crouched for another pounce. A thought crossed my mind. 'You don't think it could have – rabies, do you?'
'It's a possibility.'
And the squirrel was between us and the door.

3 Find words or phrases in the text that mean the same as the following:

    a) killing it for humane reasons
    b) nearly dead
    c) spoke very quietly
    d) looked (at us) in an angry way
    e) rise into the air
    f) the name of a terrible disease

4 Look at the verbs used to describe movement in the paragraph at the end of the text ('The squirrel ... rabies, do you?'):

levitate   power   dive   bounce   spin round   crouch

With a partner, try to decide what each one means; use your commonsense about how this type of animal might move, as well as clues in the text. Use gesture, physical movement, and diagrams or drawings to illustrate your ideas.

Now put the correct form of one of the verbs into each gap in the following sentences.

    a) The big car .... down the motorway at 100 mph.
    b) I saw a little boy .... a huge beach ball on the sand.
    c) Some Indian yogis are able to ....
    d) The girl .... into the swimming pool with a big splash.
    e) The detective heard a slight noise and .... , only to see the door bang shut and hear the key turn in the lock.
    f) The hunter .... behind a small rock, in the hope that the rhinoceros wouldn't see him.

74 ANIMALS

6 MINUTES

5 **Exam Practice**

Read the text again and answer the following multiple choice questions. Try to work out which are the distractors and discuss with a partner before giving a final answer.

1   The man with the large hands

   A   was a neighbour.
   B   had been at the bottom of the garden.
   C   did not like the wounded squirrel.
   D   did not trust the wounded squirrel.

2   When the story-teller returned upstairs, he at first thought that the squirrel was

   A   dead.
   B   paralysed.
   C   unconscious.
   D   dangerous.

6 Here is part of the text again. Without looking back at the original, try to fill each gap with one of the adverbs from the list below.

   actually   authoritatively
   suddenly   gently
   cautiously   automatically
   fixedly   miraculously

> 'I don't think so,' said the large-handed man (1) .... The squirrel glared up at us (2) .... With the benefit of hindsight, I wonder why I (3) .... assume losers are always nice.
>
> 'Perhaps it's going into a coma,' I said (4) ....
>
> 'I don't think so,' said the ham-fisted one (5) ....
>
> I moved towards it. 'I wouldn't do that, (6) ....,' he said.
>
> 'Why?'
>
> These were the last calm words that anyone uttered for some time. The squirrel (7) .... appeared to levitate as it powered towards us.
>
> 'Look out!' we both yelled as we dived in different directions.
>
> The (8) .... arisen squirrel bounced off the door between us, spun round, and crouched for another pounce. A thought crossed my mind. 'You don't think it could have – rabies, do you?'

Check your answers with the text and then make a list of adverbs of manner in the first part of the text.

7 Here is a table of common adjectives.
Can you form the adverbs? Watch out for the exceptions and pay attention to spelling.

Adjectives	Adverbs
beautiful	
good	
automatic	
slow	
bad	
happy	
fast	
comfortable	

8 Exam Practice

Finish each of the following sentences in such a way that it means exactly the same as the sentence printed before it.

a) I last had a pet when I was a child.

I haven't ....

b) I was bitten by that camel.

That's the camel ....

c) I don't think you ought to buy a dog.

It ....

d) She learnt to ride five years ago.

She's ....

e) She's very fond of her two cats.

She likes ....

f) 'Where's the zoo?' asked the children.

The children asked ....

g) We've run out of dog food.

There's ....

h) Whales live longer than human beings.

Human beings don't ....

i) Don't blame me if the puppies made a mess on the carpet.

It's not ....

j) Whose budgerigar is this?
Who does this ....

9 *In this exercise, choose the word or phrase which best completes each sentence.*

1 Please ask the children not .... the monkeys.
   A feeding   B fed   C to feed   D food

2 The tiger ran .... the deer but didn't catch it.
   A into   B after   C near   D over

3 Stay away from that dog – it could .... you!
   A bark   B kick   C bite   D howl

4 If I had realized pets could be so troublesome, I .... one.
   A did not buy   B would not buy
   C will not buy   D wouldn't have bought

5 The bird was .... of eating a worm when the cat pounced.
   A in the middle   B on its way
   C halfway through   D in the centre

6 The new zoo, ... the animals are kept in much bigger cages, is much more humane.
   A from which B by which C to which   D in which

7 The horse is .... a beautiful animal.
   A so   B enough   C too   D such

8 There are far .... elephants in Africa than there used to be.
   A fewer   B few   C lesser   D less

9 .... is an important issue – wild animals must be better protected.
   A Conserve   B Conservation C Preserve D Preservation

10 He had never .... any experience as a dog handler, but decided to take the job anyway.
   A made   B done   C had   D worked

11 I've offered a .... for the return of my missing kitten.
   A bonus   B reward   C tip   D pay

12 I watched the eagle flying away until it was out of ....
   A viewing   B vision   C the way   D sight

13 My parrot can't talk as .... as yours.
    A good   B well   C fair   D just

14 The duck-billed platypus is the .... mammal that lays eggs.
    A only   B single   C alone   D first

15 I'm going to buy a guard dog .... anyone tries to burgle my house.
    A because   B in case   C perhaps   D if only

Section B

[1] Look at these pictures.

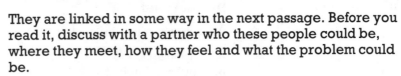

They are linked in some way in the next passage. Before you read it, discuss with a partner who these people could be, where they meet, how they feel and what the problem could be.

Now skim read the text to see if your guesses were correct.

One morning he was coming out of the bathroom at the front end of the hall, having just given Caesar his bath and rubbed him into a glow with a heavy towel. Before the door, lying in wait for him, as it were, stood a tall figure in a flowing blue silk dressing-gown that fell away from her marble arms. In her hands she carried various accessories of the bath.

'I wish,' she said distinctly, standing in his way, 'I wish you wouldn't wash your dog in the tub. I never heard of such a thing! I've found his hair in the tub, and I've smelled a doggy smell, and now I've caught you at it. It's an outrage!'

Hedger was badly frightened. She was so tall and positive, and was fairly blazing with beauty and anger. He stood blinking, holding on to his sponge and dog-soap, feeling that he ought to bow very low to her. But what he actually said was:

'Nobody has ever objected before. I always wash the tub, – and, anyhow, he's cleaner than most people.'

'Cleaner than me?' her eyebrows went up, her white arms and neck and her fragrant person seemed to scream at him like a band of outraged nymphs. Something flashed through his mind about a man who was turned into a dog, or was pursued by dogs, because he unwittingly intruded upon the bath of beauty.

'No, I didn't mean that,' he muttered, turning scarlet under the bluish stubble of his muscular jaws. 'But I know he's cleaner than I am.'

'That I don't doubt!' Her voice sounded like a soft shivering of crystal and with a smile of pity she drew the folds of her voluminous blue robe close about her and allowed the wretched man to pass. Even Caesar was frightened; he darted like a streak down the hall, through the door and to his own bed in the corner among the bones.

Hedger stood still in the doorway, listening to indignant sniffs and coughs and a great swishing of water about the sides of the tub. He had washed it; but as he had washed it with Caesar's sponge, it was quite possible that a few bristles remained; the dog was shedding now.

8 MINUTES

2 Exam Practice

Read the text again before trying to answer these multiple choice questions. As in Section A, try to work out which are the distractors and check this with a partner before giving a final answer.

1 Hedger and the girl

    A   know each other well.
    B   are old enemies.
    C   have not met before.
    D   are related.

2 When the girl complains, Hedger

    A   apologises.
    B   makes an excuse.
    C   argues.
    D   gets angry.

3   The girl

    A   was surprised that Hedger was washing his dog in the bath.
    B   knew that Hedger was washing his dog in the bath.
    C   suspected someone of washing a dog in the bath.
    D   knew that someone was washing a dog in the bath.

3 *The following sets of words and phrases will form a letter written by the girl to her mother. Make all the changes and additions necessary to produce the letter. Note carefully from the example what kind of alterations need to be made.*

New York
3rd June

Dear Mother,

Yesterday I finally discover / man who / wash / dog / bath!

a) <u>Yesterday I finally discovered the man who has been washing his dog in the bath!</u>

I wait / corridor / when he come / bathroom.

b) ....

I tell / I think / outrageous, but / not apologise.

c) ....

In fact / he suggest / dog / clean / me!

d) ....

The bathroom / stink / dog / and be dog hairs / bath.

e) ....

I have to clean / bath twice / disinfectant / before I can have / bath yesterday.

f) ....

I not know / man's name / but I know / room number.

g) ....

I write / landlord / complain.

h) ....

I wish / not come / this crazy city!

i) ....

      Please write soon,

      Lots of love,

      Eden

ANIMALS

4 *Fill each of the numbered blanks in the next part of the text. Use only **one** word in each space.*

It had never occurred to Hedger that anyone would mind using the (1) .... after Caesar; – but then, he had never seen a beautiful girl (2) .... for the bath before. As soon as he (3) .... her standing there, he (4) .... the unfitness of it. For that matter, she ought not to step into a tub that any other (5) .... had bathed in.

Section C

1 Look at the text and decide

  a) where it's from.
  b) how many different advertisements there are.

PET KEEPER AND FANCIER . . .
is a brand new animal magazine all about pets and the people that keep them; also covers every aspect of pet keeping. The magazine will have plenty of interest for the serious fancier as well as the simple pet keeper.
ORDER NOW YOUR COPY FROM YOUR LOCAL PET SHOP OR BUY BY SUBSCRIPTION FROM:
PET KEEPER & FANCIER
55 Laburnum Drive, Oswestry, Shropshire ST11 2QP

● **Exquisite fluffy white pedigree Chinchilla** Persian kittens, also superb golden Persian kittens, ready November and December, bookings taken.

● **Quality pedigree British shorthair kittens**, vaccinated adorable temperaments, beautiful colours in blue, white, cream, tortoiseshell and blue-cream, home reared by a top breeder to loving pet homes.
(T

WILTON BIRD AND EXOTIC PET CENTRE
Macaws ★ African Greys
Amazons ★ Cockatoos ★ Mynah
Birds ★ All types of small
Parrots ★ Parakeets ★ Budgies
Canaries ★ Finches ★ Quails
All types of: Lizards, Snakes, Spiders, Frogs, Terrapins, Tortoises, Monkeys, Chipmunks, Chinchillas, Rats, Mice, Rabbits and Guinea Pigs
Trade supplied
95 Pound Lane,
Bowers Gifford,
Basildon.

DOGS

● **West Highland Terriers, black Scottish Terriers and golden Retrievers**, caring professional breeder based in Aberdeenshire with a wealth of experience has quality pedigree puppies available to private responsible homes only, and will personally deliver them anywhere UK mainland to ensure they arrive safe and well and in the right home. Price including delivery, insurance, inoculation and food and feeding instructions, £185. After sales advice and past customer references in the South always available. Our puppies are genuine and so are we. Sceptics need not apply.
(T

SOUTH LONDON DOG TRAINING
We Specialise in Training Family Pets and Guard Work, also evening classes or private tuition and a qualified instructor.

DISCOUNT VIDEO SPECIALS FOR XMAS
We stock the UK's ONLY comprehensive video library for Parrot and other bird lovers. SAE for FREE list. Here are all the questions you've ever asked and more, answered by the world's leading bird breeders and avian veterinarians. We are also breeders since 1978 of 30 species of the parrot family. Babies and some adult pairs usually available. Birds also wanted for our breeding programme
PARROT PARK — the UK's original Custom Parrot service,
Holkham House Farm, Beeston, Norfolk PE32 2NJ

CORLEY DOG TRAINING CENTRE
When it comes to dog training we take the lead! **Obedience, Guard, Protection, Agility.** Top quality trained German Shepherds for sale, also puppies for show or working. Our training is the best and our prices beat the rest!

● Oriental kittens, various colours, home reared, used to dogs.

ANIMALS

● **Work with dogs.** We are looking for a person or a couple (caravan available) to help work and run the Dog Training Centre. You will have had many years experience in boarding kennels, a rudimentary knowledge of vetinary care or better. A thorough knowledge of dog training (either professionaly or as a hobby) is desirable but not essential. Please write with full details, The Dog Training Centre, Sandy Lane, Watford. WD2 8HE.

DOES YOUR DOG TAKE YOU FOR A WALK?
Then send him to us for a two week course of general obedience, any age or type, collection and delivery service available. East Anglian Dog Training Centre.

──────────────────────── (T

PORTABLE PET PENS
Indoor and outdoor, fully collapsable, sold flat, erect and dismantles in seconds, we also manufacture aviaries, cat dwellings and dog kennels. 36p sae: Avenue Aviaries (Department PP), 10/11 Potteries, Southend Lane, Waltham Abbey, Essex.

SUPER STRONG COLLARS, LEADS AND HARNESSES FOR STRONG DOGS
OPEN SUNDAYS ONLY 10 am-6 pm
26 PINFOLD ROAD, LONDON SW16
(STREATHAM)
Plus Bull Breeds books, old prints and memorabilia. Send sae for brochures

STOLEN
Two white bull terrier bitch puppies, 11 weeks old, one has red left ear, the other brindle right ear. substantial reward offered.

● **Love is a Monterosa St.Bernard puppy**, the great dog with the great temperament. Information freely given by long experienced breeder, puppies usually available. Monterosa Kennels, Hopton, Nr Diss, Norfolk.
(T

  2 Exam Practice

Now answer the following multiple choice questions.

1   There are

   A   four adverts trying to sell dogs.
   B   as many adverts trying to sell cats as there are for dogs.
   C   three places advertising dog training.
   D   two magazines specially for dog lovers.

2   Parrot Park

   A   gives you a free video with every parrot you buy.
   B   began making videos in 1978.
   C   only answers questions about parrots.
   D   buys and sells parrots.

3   If you want the job as a dog trainer you must

   A   be trained as a vet.
   B   have a lot of experience in looking after dogs.
   C   have a lot of experience in training dogs.
   D   have a caravan.

3 *The following sets of words and phrases will form a letter of application for the job as a dog trainer. Make any changes and additions necessary to produce the complete letter. Note carefully from the example what kind of alterations need to be made.*

London
20th February

Dear Sir/Madam,

I / like / apply / job / advertise / 'Exchange and Mart' magazine / 16th February.

a) *I would like to apply for the job advertised in 'Exchange and Mart' on 16th February.*

I / work / dogs / over ten years.

b) ....

I start / career / manage / own kennels / Scotland.

c) ....

Four years ago I become / dog trainer / local police.

d) ....

I now want / move / London area.

e) ....

In your reply please indicate / salary and conditions of employment.

f) ....

I / not need / accommodation.

g) ....

I / available / interview / any time.

h) ....

I look forward / hearing you.

i) ....

Yours faithfully,

David Philips

4 Do you think the man who wrote this letter would get the job? Why/why not? Make a list of reasons and discuss with a partner. Would you like this job?

5 Exam Practice

Look at these pictures of pets.
Decide which one each of the following people would choose and give your reasons. Write a paragraph of about 50 words for each person.

i. Sarah
    Age: 27   She is a doctor.   She is single and lives in a small flat in the centre of the city.

ii. Peter and Louise
    They are in their thirties with a young family. They have a house in the country and Peter works on a farm nearby. Louise is a freelance journalist.

iii. Adam
    Age: 14   He lives with his parents in a small house in the suburbs.

iv. Mrs Harris
    Age: 74   She's a widow and confined to a wheelchair.

The best pet for Sarah ....
....

I would advise Mrs. Harris ....
....

Peter and Louise should ....
....

And finally, ...
....

6 *The word in capitals at the end of each of the following sentences can be used to form a word that fits suitably in the blank space. Fill each blank in this way.*

a) Large dogs must be treated properly or they can become ....
   DANGER

b) My puppy was so .... when I bought him that I had to take him to training classes for a year!
   OBEDIENCE

c) All the animals loved her because of her ....
   KIND

d) As he was crossing a field, a large black bull began to move towards him menacingly. .... , he jumped over the fence and got away.
   LUCK

e) One of the most amazing natural occurrences is the .... of millions of birds over vast distances every year.
   MIGRATE

f) The small orange cat rubbed itself .... against my leg.
   LOVE

g) The mosquito net he used in Africa was completely .... He woke up each morning covered in bites.
   EFFECT

h) Some fish can survive at enormous .... due to their ability to produce their own fluorescent light.
   DEEP

STUDY HINTS

Do you know what Papers 1 and 3 of the exam look like?
Have you seen any past papers?
If you haven't, you are at a serious disadvantage. It is important to

a) be totally familiar with exam paper layout and question types.

b) work through three or four of the most recent papers to know exactly what to expect.

c) try sitting at least one 'mock' exam (i.e. do the papers under strict exam conditions). Discuss this with your teacher.

Unit 8   Health

Section A

15 MINUTES

1 Read the following text and, working with a partner, try to guess what the missing words might be.

> When examining (1) .... in their beds at home, I was always coming across odd potatoes between the sheets and sometimes a pocket magnet or piece of camphor in the (2) .... pocket. For warts (3) .... was a battery of recommended treatments, but most people (4) .... until the fair came for the summer carnival, when the gypsy fortune-teller would charm the warts away. Spiders' webs (5) .... put on cuts: these did help the blood to clot, but were also likely (6) .... infect the wound with a hefty dose of bacteria.
>
> I once went out to an isolated farm to find the (7) .... with an infected, almost gangrenous, leg covered with a dressing of mouldy bread.
>
> 'What on earth have you put that stuff on his leg for?' I (8) ....
>
> 'Oh doctor,' said the farmer's wife, 'we always keep a (9) .... of mouldy rye bread in the ceiling rafter for infected cuts.'
>
> 'These old wives' tales will be the death of all of you,' I said. I was (10) ....
>
> I had to admit the farmer to hospital, where he was found to be diabetic. He had a long spell on (11) .... insulin and penicillin before we were able to get his leg into good enough shape for him to go (12) .... to his farm.
>
> Talking to Steve about this patient one morning at coffee, I said, 'When will these people (13) .... learn? Fancy putting mouldy bread on infected cuts.'
>
> Steve said, 'Don't you be (14) .... hasty with them, Bob. Mouldy bread has cured more infected cuts than it has let go bad. These people discovered penicillin long before Sir Alexander Fleming did. The mould on that bread is mainly penicillin mould: it's been used in this way for some hundreds of years. And it's not (15) .... old mouldy bread; it's good rye bread, hung up in the rafters where it's well ventilated.'
>
> He laughed. 'I will agree with you, it's a bit out of date now, but belief in the treatment plus a bit of medication goes a long way towards a cure.'

HEALTH

10 MINUTES — **2 Exam Practice**

Here is the complete text. Read it to check your answers to question 1 and to do the multiple choice questions that follow.

> When examining patients in their beds at home, I was always coming across odd potatoes between the sheets and sometimes a pocket magnet or piece of camphor in the pyjama pocket. For warts there was a battery of recommended treatments, but most people waited until the fair came for the summer carnival, when the gypsy fortune-teller would charm the warts away. Spiders' webs were put on cuts: these did help the blood to clot, but were also likely to infect the wound with a hefty dose of bacteria.
>
> I once went out to an isolated farm to find the farmer with an infected, almost gangrenous, leg covered with a dressing of mouldy bread.
>
> 'What on earth have you put that stuff on his leg for?' I asked.
>
> 'Oh doctor,' said the farmer's wife, 'we always keep a loaf of mouldy rye bread in the ceiling rafter for infected cuts.'
>
> 'These old wives' tales will be the death of all of you,' I said. I was furious.
>
> I had to admit the farmer to hospital, where he was found to be diabetic. He had a long spell on both insulin and penicillin before we were able to get his leg into good enough shape for him to go back to his farm.
>
> Talking to Steve about this patient one morning at coffee, I said, 'When will these people ever learn? Fancy putting mouldy bread on infected cuts.'
>
> Steve said, 'Don't you be too hasty with them, Bob. Mouldy bread has cured more infected cuts than it has let go bad. These people discovered penicillin long before Sir Alexander Fleming did. The mould on that bread is mainly penicillin mould: it's been used in this way for some hundreds of years. And it's not any old mouldy bread; it's good rye bread, hung up in the rafters where it's well ventilated.
>
> He laughed. 'I will agree with you, it's a bit out of date now, but belief in the treatment plus a bit of medication goes a long way towards a cure.'

1   People believed that warts

    A could only be treated by a fortune-teller.
    B could only be treated by a doctor.
    C could be treated in several ways.
    D were difficult to get rid of.

2   When the writer arrived at the farm he

    A was surprised to see the bread on the farmer's leg.
    B was angry because he thought the farmer's wife was trying to kill her husband.
    C was pleased to see them trying to help.
    D was shocked at their ignorance of medical treatment.

3   Steve thinks that

    A most cuts treated with mouldy bread get infected.
    B only some types of mouldy bread are suitable.

C   the best bread to use is 100 years old.
D   mouldy bread is bad for cuts.

3 There are some words from the text which may be new to you. Can you match them to the correct definition?

a) to clot (v.)   1) quick to judge
b) rafter (n.)   2) traditional, fictitious belief
c) old wives' tale (n.)   3) bandage
d) hasty (adj.)   4) to become very thick
e) dressing (n.)   5) piece of wood in the ceiling

4 Do you know any 'old wives' tales' from your own country? Discuss them with a partner and then with your group. Are any of them based on fact as in this story?

5 Exam Practice

Finish each of the following sentences in such a way that it means exactly the same as the sentence printed before it.

a)   Science still hasn't found a cure for the common cold.

     A cure for the common cold ....

b)   It's not necessary for you to stay in bed.

     You ....

c)   Although she had just had an operation, Jo still went skiing.

     In spite of ....

d)   I don't like it when you smoke at the table.

     I wish ....

e)   It took me two hours to run round the park!

     I spent ....

f)   The doctor warned him that his heavy drinking was killing him.

     'If you ....

g)   The ambulance arrived too late to save his life.

     By the time ....

h)   This diet is great!

     What ....

i)   I didn't like the way he used to worry about trivial things.

     He was ....

HEALTH

Section B

1 What do you know about the effects of smoking?

e.g. How addictive is nicotine?
How long does it take for the effects to wear off?
What effects (good and bad) does it have on the body?

2 Now scan the text and put a ___ next to things you put on your list, a ___ next to things you knew but didn't put on your list, and a ___ next to things you didn't know.

To do this effectively, you probably need

a) 5 seconds.
b) 2 minutes.
c) 5 minutes.
d) 10 minutes.

SMOKING

Nicotine is as addictive as heroin. Its hooks go deep, involving complex physiological and psychological mechanisms that drive and maintain the smoker.

Like heroin, nicotine is an alkaloid found in plants. The alkaloid kills insects by disrupting their neurotransmitters – substances released by the bugs' activated nerve cells. Humans have the same neurotransmitters. But what is toxic to a bug is pleasurable to the human when taken in the small amounts contained in cigarettes. Heroin attaches itself to the natural painkilling receptors, but nicotine affects the major neurotransmitter system which conducts nerve signals, memory and their critical functions. Once in the body it is carried within seconds to most body tissues by binding itself to white blood cells.

But nicotine differs from other addictive drugs in several ways:
• Its effects are felt more rapidly than drugs taken intravenously. One quarter of the nicotine in each drag reaches the brain in seven seconds. The nicotine concentration in the blood peaks at about the time the cigarette butt is extinguished. The effects fall off rapidly as the nicotine is cleared by the liver and excreted in the urine.

Within half an hour most smokers are reaching for another cigarette. A pack-a-day smoker takes 70,000 drug 'hits' a year.
• Nicotine does not interfere with normal activity.

The smoker uses nicotine to fine-tune the body's reactions to the world and is incredibly adept at maintaining a steady concentration of nicotine in the bloodstream throughout the day. There is an internal sensing system, something like a heating thermostat, which knows when nicotine levels are too low. It prompts a smoker to light up when the nicotine level needs boosting. Most smokers need a minimum of ten cigarettes to maintain a comfortable threshold. Watch a cigarette addict drawing on his first cigarette of the day. He will inhale the smoke deeply to lift fallen nicotine levels.

Nicotine improves short-term memory and gives subjective relief from stress, while at the same time inducing the biological symptoms of stress by speeding up the heart rate and raising blood pressure. A smoker's heartbeat is increased about eight to ten beats a minute all day and night – producing excessive wear on the heart. It's not only the nicotine in a cigarette that causes trouble, but everything else that goes with it – the tar, the carbon monoxide and thousands of poisons that find their way into the lungs and then around the body – which can also contribute to life-threatening problems, such as heart and lung disease.

Research shows that nicotine withdrawal symptoms include

anxiety, irritability, lack of concentration, cravings, drowsiness, decreased heart rate, tremors and slowed metabolism. The smoker who wants to kick the habit needs a great deal of support and will only succeed, say the experts, if he or she really *wants* to. Feeling that you *ought* to isn't reason enough.

The hard facts of smoking
Smoking kills over 100,000 people in the UK each year.
In 1987, 44,546 people died of heart disease directly caused by smoking. Approximately 36,000 people die from lung cancer and a further 25,714 people die from bronchitis and emphysema caused by smoking.

Women smokers are three and a half times more likely to suffer cervical cancer.
Smoking is implicated in male and female infertility.
Smokers give birth to babies that are usually 200g smaller than average and remain underweight until early adulthood.

3 If you are a smoker, have you ever tried to give up? Why/why not?
If you're not a smoker, do you know anyone who smokes who has tried to give up?
Were you/they successful? Why/why not?
Discuss these questions with a partner.

10 MINUTES

4 **Exam Practice**

Read the text again and answer the following multiple choice questions.

1　Heroin and nicotine are

　　A　pleasing for insects and humans.
　　B　used as painkillers.
　　C　not very addictive.
　　D　produced by plants as a defence against insects.

2　There is most nicotine in the blood

　　A　seven seconds after smoking a cigarette.
　　B　about half an hour after smoking a cigarette.
　　C　as the smoker finishes the cigarette.
　　D　at the beginning of the cigarette.

HEALTH

3   Levels of nicotine in the blood of smokers are

   A   constant throughout the day.
   B   raised when the body gets hot.
   C   highest in the morning.
   D   highest in the evening.

4   Smoking

   A   causes heart disease by underworking the heart muscles.
   B   is one of the causes of infertility.
   C   makes people feel irritable and stressed.
   D   makes pregnant mothers lose weight.

5 *Fill each space in the following sentences with* **one** *appropriate word connected with the subject of* **health**. *(The words can be found in the text.)*

1   I had no idea that smoking was so .... I always thought I could give up whenever I wanted to, but I'm actually finding it very difficult.
2   Smoking is one of the major causes of lung .... and heart ....
3   The nurse gave the boy with the broken arm a .... so that it wouldn't hurt so much.
4   I told the doctor all my .... and he said that I probably had some kind of terrible tropical disease.
5   When you do very vigorous exercise, the amount of oxygen in the .... goes up and you feel better.

6 *Here is a conversation between two colleagues in a canteen at work. Fill in the missing parts.*

A: Cigarette?

B: No ....

A: Very wise of you. I wish I didn't.

B: Have .... ?

A: Yes; three or four times.

B: When .... ?

A: About three or four months ago actually.

B: So, what .... ?

A: Well, it was okay for about a week or so and then I was at a party, and you know how it is. You get talking and before you know it you've got a cigarette in your mouth.

B: How .... ?

A: Erm ... a couple of packets a day.

B: You .... !
A: Yes, that's why I'd like to stop or at least cut down.
B: Why .... ?
A: That's a good idea! Do you think it would work?

7 *Nicki (22 years old) is a language student living in London. She has found a two-bedroom flat to rent and is looking for someone to share. She puts this advertisement in the newspaper and on the college noticeboard.*

> **FLATMATE WANTED**
>
> Large room in cosy flat to let.
> Shared kitchen and bath.
> Non-smoking female preferred.
> Must be tidy and quiet.
>
> Tel: 562 2140

Using the information below, write three paragraphs of about 60 words each, saying which people would be the most suitable flat mates for Nicki.

a) John (25) – Laboratory technician. Non-smoker. Not a very tidy person.

b) Margaret (18) – Secretary. Non-smoker. Loves discos, parties and late nights.

c) Sarah (21) – English Literature student. Light smoker.

d) Mary (27) – Bio-chemist. Non-smoker. Has a pet dog.

Her first choice could be ....
....

Her second choice could be ....
....

Her third choice might be ....
....

92 HEALTH

Section C

1 Do you mind going to the dentist?

With a partner, discuss your feelings about dentists.

2 Draw a diagram of your mouth and label it with the following words:

teeth   gums   lips   tongue

Can you draw a diagram of a tooth as well?

With a partner, and using your diagrams, describe what happens to your teeth if you don't clean them.

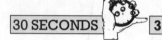

3 Now look at the text below and decide if it is from
  a) a newspaper.
  b) a public information leaflet.
  c) an advertisement for toothpaste.
  d) a medical textbook.

Dental Disease.

Dental disease means tooth decay and gum disease.

TOOTH DECAY.

Decay occurs when teeth are decalcified by acid. This acid is formed from the breakdown of sugar by the bacteria in PLAQUE, a colourless sticky film mainly composed of bacteria, which collects on teeth and gums. The sugar most commonly eaten is sucrose, and this is the worst offender.

The graph below shows the way acidity of the mouth is changed by eating sugar and it is obvious that it is the number of times during the day that the "danger zone" is entered that is important, not the quantity of sugar eaten each time.

The quantity of sugar will however be decreased by decreasing the frequency of sugar intake, (for your guidance a choice of safe substitute snacks is listed on page 7 of this leaflet).

Brushing after eating is ineffective because the decalcification starts too quickly and because brushing is often inefficient at plaque removal. Moreover, to suggest brushing after meals is confusing since the objective of brushing is to remove plaque – not miscellaneous food debris.

Ending a meal with cheese is however a good idea – since it has the effect of depressing acid levels.

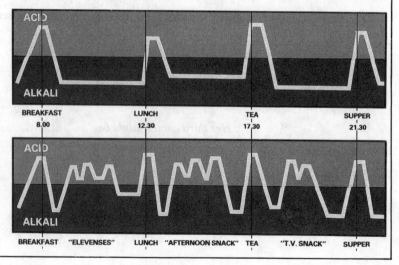

SUGAR + BACTERIA = ACID

ACID + ENAMEL = DECAY

HEALTH

4 Exam Practice

Now answer these multiple choice questions.

1. Tooth decay

    A   happens whenever you eat sugar.
    B   only happens when you eat sucrose.
    C   is a transparent substance that attacks teeth and gums.
    D   is a result of sugar attacking your teeth.

2. It is better to

    A   avoid acidic food.
    B   eat less, more often.
    C   eat more, less often.
    D   avoid eating so often.

3. According to the leaflet, brushing your teeth

    A   is a waste of time.
    B   doesn't really get rid of plaque.
    C   is most useful after eating cheese.
    D   should be done immediately after a meal.

5

*Fill each of the numbered blanks in the following text from another part of the leaflet. Use only **one** word in each space.*

GUM DISEASE

Gum disease is (1) .... biggest single cause of tooth loss. Plaque and bacteria not (2) .... help cause decay, but the toxins which they (3) .... cause inflammation – this is the first stage of gum disease.

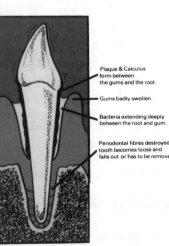

Plaque & Calculus form between the gums and the root.
Gums badly swollen.
Bacteria extending deeply between the root and gum.
Periodontal fibres destroyed, tooth becomes loose and falls out or has to be removed.

(4) .... the plaque hardens and calcifies into calculus (or tartar) further layers of plaque (5) .... deposited. This solidified film is no longer removable (6) .... normal brushing and can only be removed effectively by a dentist.

Gum disease is prevented by removing plaque.

Removing plaque needs a good technique. That is any technique that (7) .... remove the plaque completely (8) .... damaging the gums.

How do you know when the plaque (9) .... gone?

Plaque is (10) .... invisible, but with the aid of simple food dyes (11) .... disclosing tablets (available at most chemists') it (12) .... be quite dramatically demonstrated. All the stained plaque can then be removed with a soft, multi-tufted small headed brush (13) .... good condition.

It is far (14) .... beneficial to do this thoroughly once each day, (15) .... than make three cursory attempts.

15 MINUTES

6 *In this exercise, choose the word or phrase which best completes each sentence.*

1 To my ...., my darling husband's illness was less serious than I had thought.
   A view   B judgement   C relief   D dismay

2 You've gone as white as a sheet – do you .... faint?
   A going to   B feel   C become   D stay

3 The seafood I had for dinner has given me ....
   A infection   B indigestion   C sickness   D indisposition

4 The consultation was .... reassuring, but she still felt the surgeon could have given her more advice.
   A completely   B exactly   C quite   D totally

5 Many people are .... to insect bites, and some even have to go to hospital.
   A insensitive   B allergic   C sensible   D infected

6 '................ please, and I'll put you through to the ambulance service.'
   A Ring up   B Hang up   C Hang on   D Ring off

7 I'm .... trying to give up smoking but I haven't succeeded yet.
   A ever   B usually   C sometimes   D always

8 You'll have a nervous breakdown .... you stop worrying so much.
   A if   B when   C unless   D until

9 Ingrid came back from a holiday in Thailand with a very .... disease and couldn't go back to work for a month.
   A insidious   B constant   C contagious   D infected

10 Fresh fruit is very good for you and .... are green vegetables.
   A even   B so   C too   D also

HEALTH 95

11 If only I .... give up smoking.
    A could   B would   C should   D can

12 You .... take some aspirins if you've got a bad headache.
    A better   B will   C rather   D should

13 .... from John we're all vegetarians in this house, for health reasons.
    A Unless   B Apart   C Except   D Besides

14 It is very important to keep all medicines well out of the .... of small children.
    A hands   B stretch   C reach   D touch

15 Good health .... on good eating habits, plenty of exercise and not too much worry!
    A lies   B depends   C rests   D goes

16 You should visit your doctor at least once a year for ....
    A an inspection   B a check up
    C a control   D an investigation

HEALTH

17 Exceeding the stated .... of some medicines can result in death.
    A measure   B allowance   C dose   D pills

18 My tooth is giving me a lot of .... I hope the dentist can do something for me.
    A ill   B sick   C pain   D hurt

19 She's .... better — another few days in bed should do the trick.
    A fairly   B almost   C just   D completely

20 My boss is taking early retirement .... ill health.
    A on account of   B in front of
    C on behalf of   D ahead of

7 *The following sets of words and phrases will form a letter written by a woman in hospital. Make all the changes and additions necessary to produce the letter. Note carefully from the example what kind of alterations need to be made.*

Tooting General Hospital
19th December

Dear Peggy,

This / short note / thank you / flowers / send me.

a) *This is just a short note to thank you for the flowers you sent me.*

I still / hospital / after have / six teeth take out, and I / never be / such pain.

b) ....

If I have / children / I make sure / they clean / teeth more often / I do.

c) ....

I wish I not eat / many sweets / I be young.

d) ....

Now I not have / teeth / eat with!

e) ....

Anyway, it be lovely / see you / if you not be too busy.

f) ....

Thanks again / flowers.

g) ....

Jennifer

HEALTH 97

> **STUDY HINTS**
> Vocabulary you have particular difficulty remembering will need special attention. The best way to remember something is to make it memorable. There are many ways of doing this, and you will need to experiment to find out which is most suitable for you. Here are some suggestions.

- Write words on pieces of paper and then put them or stick them in ridiculous places:

  in the fridge   in the collar of your favourite jacket
  on top of the TV   on the dog's collar
  on your toothbrush   on your knife and fork
  in the fruit bowl   on the bathroom mirror

- Buy a small notebook, or set aside part of your regular vocabulary notebook and label it 'Topics'.

  Choose a topic you like and write it in the centre of the page:

  Write down the first word you can think of connected with the topic and join it to the topic word with a line. If you don't know the English for the word, look it up in a dictionary.

  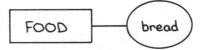

  Carry on like this, adding new words as you go. You can continue to add words after a few days or even a few months. Each time you add something, you will be revising all the words you wrote down before by looking at the network again. Make sure that you can still remember what they all mean.

  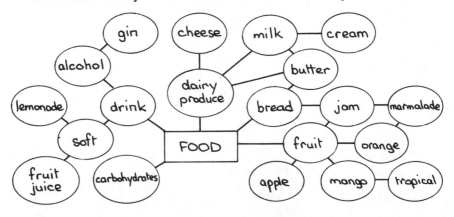

- When you are sitting on the bus or train, try to think of words which have things in common:

    roar howl squeak growl (animal noises)
    unhappy untidy unnecessary unadventurous (prefix)

    When you arrive home, write down as many of the groups as you can remember.

- Cut out useful words from newspapers or magazines and make a collage with them. Stick it up on your bedroom wall, or take it into your class and encourage your friends to do the same. You could have a competition for the best collage.

- Write down words you want to learn on separate pieces of card, with a translation, a picture or an example sentence on the back.
  Put them into a small bag or a box.
  Take them out one at a time and see if you can remember the meaning. If you can, put them into another bag or box labelled 'Words I Know'. If you can't, put them back and try again later. Every week, check that you can still remember the meaning of the words in the 'Words I Know' bag and, if you can't, transfer them back to the first bag.

- Write crosswords for your friends, and get them to write crosswords for you, using words you have just studied in class.

Unit 9 Jobs

Section A

1 Look at this headline:

> # He's suffering from multiple fractures. His family are suffering from shock.

Decide if it is from

a) a newspaper article.
b) an advert.
c) a textbook.

Discuss your choice with a partner and try to guess what the text will be about.

1 MINUTE

2 Now skim the text to see if you were right.

HE'S SUFFERING FROM MULTIPLE FRACTURES.
HIS FAMILY ARE SUFFERING FROM SHOCK.

There are times when relatives need just as much care as patients.

In this case, a boy's motorcycle accident has turned his whole family into casualties. And suddenly as a nurse you have three people to care for instead of one.

Of course, the patient's welfare is of paramount importance. But it would be your job not only to look after him, but also to treat his parents with the right degree of honesty and tact, answering their questions sensitively.

Contrary to popular belief, nursing isn't only about taking blood pressures and giving injections.

A nurse needs more than just technical skills. She or he needs interpersonal skills as well.

Nursing is about caring for the whole person. Emotionally as well as physically. A nurse, therefore, will be concerned with everything and anything that might affect a patient's recovery.

That's why a nurse's training takes place in clinical areas as well as the classroom.

Only by gaining practical experience will you learn many of the attributes needed to be a good nurse.

You'll learn how to deal with all sorts of patients. (From the sweetly reasonable to the occasionally abusive.) You'll learn how to keep cool, calm and collected in an emergency – the last thing a patient wants to see is a nurse getting flustered.

And you'll also learn how rewarding it is to see a patient gradually recover and eventually walk out of the hospital fit and well again.

Talking of rewards, what about pay?

A Registered General Nurse (RGN) on an orthopaedic ward with three years' experience could expect to earn £9,175 a year. And in Inner London an extra £1,800 on top of that. (This excludes unsocial hours payment.)

In terms of prospects the sky's the limit.

In a few short years you could be a Ward Sister or Charge Nurse or in a more senior clinical post. You could even go into management, teaching or research.

Naturally, as you go up the ladder, your salary will also go up. To find out more, fill in and send off the coupon or phone.

WHAT DID YOU DO AT WORK TODAY?

Please send me your Nursing Careers Pack. (TICK AS APPLICABLE)

I am 17 or under ☐   18-24 ☐   25-34 ☐   35 or over ☐

I have 1-4 GCSE/'O' level or equivalent passes ☐

I have 5 or more GCSE/'O' level or equivalent passes ☐

Not applicable/Exams not yet taken ☐

NAME
(Mr/Mrs/Miss/Ms)   (USE BLOCK CAPITALS)
ADDRESS

POSTCODE   TELEPHONE

Send coupon to NURSING RDST2, FREEPOST, Brentford, Middlesex TW8 8BR, or phone FREE anytime
0800 333 666. **NURSING**

[3] Write down five adjectives describing the qualities required to be a nurse.

e.g. honest, tactful

[4] **Exam Practice**

Read the text again and answer the multiple choice questions.

1. Most people think that

    A nursing is mainly a technical profession.
    B nurses are overworked because they have too many people to look after.
    C nurses never tell lies to patients.
    D nurses only look after the patients.

2. The most important qualities of a good nurse are

    A being emotional and sensitive.
    B getting flustered in an emergency.
    C not being abusive to some patients.
    D thinking about the patient's emotional state as well as his/her physical one.

3. An RGN in central London with 4 years' experience could be earning

    A as much as £9,175.
    B up to £10,975.
    C under £9,175.
    D over £10,975.

4. The advert

    A says that promotion is automatic with experience.
    B warns that promotion prospects are limited.
    C implies that promotion prospects are good.
    D says that promotion is difficult to get but well paid.

[5] Would you like to be a nurse?
Why/why not? Discuss your reasons with a partner and make a list of the advantages and disadvantages of this job to discuss with the rest of the group.

JOBS

6 **Exam Practice**

The following sets of words and phrases will form a letter asking for an interview, from a girl who is interested in becoming a nurse. Make any changes or additions necessary to produce the complete letter. Note carefully from the example what kind of alterations need to be made.

Manchester
May 21st

Dear Sir/Madam,

Thank you / Nursing Careers Pack / receive / last week.

a) Thank you for the Nursing Careers Pack which I received last week.

I / final year / school / and / finish / exams / summer.

b) ....

I like / start nursing / following October.

c) ....

possible / arrange / interview / this month, or / I have to wait / next year?

d) ....

I be sorry / application / bit late, / please give / full consideration.

e) ....

I not want / waste / year / work / shop!

f) ....

I look forward / hearing you.

g) ....

Yours faithfully,

Ms S. Hunter

---

7 *The word in capitals at the end of each of the following sentences can be used to form a word that fits suitably in the blank space. Fill each blank in this way.*

a) The .... rate is coming down at last. More people will be able to find jobs now. **EMPLOY**

b) You need to get good .... in order to be a doctor. **QUALIFY**

c) The last .... was selected for the job because she had more experience than the others. **INTERVIEW**

d) When applying for a job, it's important to fill in the .... form properly. **APPLY**

e) Most people continue working until 60 or 65, but recently people have been taking early .... **RETIRE**

f) The company had to close down because its prices were not .... **COMPETE**

g) .... developments mean that we don't have to work so hard — most of the thinking is now done by computers. **TECHNOLOGY**

h) Computers have .... our lives; they can do everything from mathematics to making cars! **REVOLUTION**

i) Job .... is very important if you're going to do the same thing for most of your adult life. **SATISFY**

j) I'm in a terrible state — .... and with nowhere to live. **JOB**

Section B

15 MINUTES

1 Look at the text and try to fill in the missing words.

Waiting briefly for the lift he told (1) .... that he was no more involved than he would be in any other case. Berowne was dead. It was his business to find out (2) .... and why. Commitment was to the job, to the living, (3) .... to the dead.

He had hardly passed (4) .... the swing doors when Massingham (5) .... up the ramp with the Rover. (6) .... in beside him Dalgliesh asked:

'Fingerprints and photography, they're on (7) .... way?'

'Yes, sir.'

'And the lab?'

'They're sending a senior biologist. She'll meet (8) .... there.'

(9) '................ you manage to get Doctor Kynaston?'

'No, sir, only the housekeeper. He's been in New England visiting his daughter. He always goes there in the autumn. He was due back at Heathrow (10) .... BA flight 214 arriving at seven twenty-five. It's (11) .... , but he's probably stuck on the Westway.'

'Keep on trying his home (12) .... he arrives.'

'Doc Greeley is available, sir. Kynaston (13) .... be jet-lagged.'

'I want Kynaston, jet-lagged or not.'

Massingham said:

'Only the (14) .... for this cadaver.'

Something in (15) .... voice, a tinge of amusement, even contempt, irritated Dalgliesh. He thought, my God, am I getting over-sensitive (16) .... this death even before I've seen the body? He fastened his (17) .... belt without speaking and the Rover slid gently (18) .... Broadway, the road he had crossed less (19) .... a fortnight earlier on his way to (20) .... Sir Paul Berowne.

 **2** **Exam Practice**

Here is the complete text. Read it to check your answers to question 1 and to do the multiple choice questions that follow.

Waiting briefly for the lift he told himself that he was no more involved than he would be in any other case. Berowne was dead. It was his business to find out how and why. Commitment was to the job, to the living, not to the dead.

He had hardly passed through the swing doors when Massingham drove up the ramp with the Rover. Getting in beside him Dalgliesh asked:

'Fingerprints and photography, they're on their way?'

'Yes, sir.'

'And the lab?'

'They're sending a senior biologist. She'll meet us there.'

'Did you manage to get Doctor Kynaston?'

'No, sir, only the housekeeper. He's been in New England visiting his daughter. He always goes there in the autumn. He was due back at Heathrow on BA flight 214 arriving at seven twenty-five. It's landed, but he's probably stuck on the Westway.'

'Keep on trying his home until he arrives.'

'Doc Greeley is available, sir. Kynaston will be jet-lagged.'

'I want Kynaston, jet-lagged or not.'

Massingham said:

'Only the best for this cadaver.'

Something in his voice, a tinge of amusement, even contempt, irritated Dalgliesh. He thought, my God, am I getting over-sensitive about this death even before I've seen the body? He fastened his seat belt without speaking and the Rover slid gently into Broadway, the road he had crossed less than a fortnight earlier on his way to see Sir Paul Berowne.

1   Dalgliesh is

    A   a photographer.
    B   a police detective.
    C   a private detective.
    D   a biologist.

2   Doctor Kynaston

    A   has a housekeeper who is in New England.
    B   is a pilot for British Airways.
    C   is married.
    D   is better than Dr. Greeley.

3   Massingham

    A   is Dalgliesh's superior.
    B   is a taxi driver.
    C   is a woman.
    D   works for the police.

4   Sir Paul Berowne

    A   was liked by Dalgliesh.
    B   had met Dalgliesh.
    C   was Dalgliesh's boss.
    D   owned a Rover.

3 A   *Fill each space in the following sentences with* **one** *appropriate word connected with the subject of* **jobs**.

1   She was the best of the five .... at the interview, so we offered her the job.
2   She wanted to take the job, but the .... was so low she couldn't afford to.
3   He was warned that if he was late again he would get the ....
4   He didn't .... until he reached the age of 75, and then he spent many happy years writing his autobiography.
5   She worked as a secretary for 10 years before she was .... to the post of office manager.

B   *Complete these sentences with a phrase made from* **put**.

1   He .... with a low salary and long hours because he loved his job.
2   The meeting has been .... until next Thursday because the chairman is sick.
3   Profits were so large that the company was able to .... the wages by 12%.

4   If you come to the interview, we'll pay your travelling expenses and .... you .... in a hotel.
5   They .... me .... a really difficult interview; I don't think I've got the job.

4   *A woman is phoning the police to report a missing child. Complete the dialogue.*

A: Hello. Is that the police station?

B: Yes, Madam. Can ....?

A: Yes. I'd like to report a missing child.

B: Could ....?

A: Er. Mrs Beryl Oakes.

B: And ....?

A: 48, Acacia Avenue, Worcester Park, Surrey.

B: Are ....?

A: No, I'm a neighbour. The mother is too upset to come to the phone.

B: Could you ....?

A: Yes, of course. It's Mrs Sally Peterson. And the child's name is Tracey Ann Peterson. They live at number 46.

B: Do you know ....?

A: Yes. She's five and a half.

B: And could ....?

A: She's got shoulder-length blonde hair, bright blue eyes and she was wearing a red jumper, black jeans and pink tennis shoes.

B: When ....?

A: About 11.30 this morning. She was playing with my children at the back of the house.

B: Could I ....?

A: Yes, it's 330-5181.

B: We'll ....

A: Thank you.

5 *Finish each of the following sentences in such a way that it means exactly the same as the sentence printed before it.*

a) Sharon lost her job because she was always late.

   If ....

b) My life isn't as exciting as yours.

   Your life ....

c) The job was so interesting that he accepted a low salary.

   It was ....

d) The Queen is the richest woman in the world.

   No other woman ....

e) Henry couldn't buy the BMW because he didn't have enough money.

   The BMW was ....

f) 'They've all been given a pay rise', said the boss.

   The boss said that ....

g) Caroline regretted leaving her job at the bank.

   'I wish ....

h) He'd prefer to lie in bed all day.

   He'd rather ....

i) If you don't get more customers, your business will collapse.

   Unless ....

j) You have to study for at least six years to become an accountant.

   It takes ....

Section C

10 MINUTES

1 **Exam Practice**

Read the text and then answer the multiple choice questions that follow.

'When I first opened the shop, all the neighbourhood kids came in. They either demanded that I "gi' them a penny"' – I hated whites' imitation of the Black accent – 'or play records for them. I explained that the only way I'd give them anything was if they worked for it and that I'd play records for their parents, but not for them until they were tall enough to reach the turntables.'

'So I let them fold empty record boxes for a penny apiece.' She went on, 'I'm glad to see you because I want to offer you a job.'

I had done many things to make a living, but I drew the line at cleaning white folks' houses. I had tried that and lasted only one day. The waxed tables, cut flowers, closets of other people's clothes totally disoriented me. I hated the figured carpets, tiled kitchens and refrigerators filled with someone else's dinner leftovers.

'Really?' The ice in my voice turned my accent to upper-class Vivien Leigh (before *Gone With the Wind*).

'My sister has been helping me in the shop, but she's going back to school. I thought you'd be perfect to take her place.'

My resolve began to knuckle under me like weak knees.

'I don't know if you know it, but I have a large clientele and try to keep in stock a supply, however small, of every record by Negro artists. And if I don't have something, there's a comprehensive catalog and I can order it. What do you think?'

Her face was open and her smile simple. I pried into her eyes for hidden meaning and found nothing. Even so, I had to show my own strength.

'I don't like to hear white folks imitate Negroes. Did the children really ask you to "gi' them a penny"? Oh, come now.'

She said, 'You are right – they didn't ask. They demanded that I "gi' them a penny." The smile left her face. 'You say it.'

'Give me a penny.' My teeth pressed my bottom lip, stressing the *v*.

She reached for the box and handed me a coin. 'Don't forget that you've been to school and let neither of us forget that we're both grown-up. I'd be pleased if you'd take the job.' She told me the salary, the hours and what my duties would be.

'Thank you very much for the offer. I'll think about it.' I left the shop, head up, back straight. I tried to exude indifference, like octopus ink, to camouflage my excitement.

1   The conversation is between

    A   two black women.
    B   two white women.
    C   one black and one white woman.
    D   one white woman and one black child.

2   The writer

    A   is suspicious of the shop-keeper's motives.
    B   is eager to take the job.
    C   feels she is too upper-class to take the job.
    D   has weak knees.

3   The shop-keeper gives the writer a coin

    A   because she's sorry for her.
    B   as an advance on her salary.
    C   because she says 'give' instead of 'gi'.
    D   as a friendly gesture.

4   The shop-keeper thinks the writer's pronunciation is different from the black children's because

    A   she's an adult.
    B   she's educated.
    C   she's angry.
    D   she's only pretending to speak differently.

2 *The following sets of words and phrases will form a letter. It is from the writer of the passage to her friend, after she has been working in the shop for a couple of weeks. Make all the changes and additions necessary to produce the complete letter. Note carefully from the example what kind of alterations need to be made.*

Dear Ella,

I do / new job / two weeks / I like / very much.

a)   I've been doing my new job for two weeks and I like it very much.

I start / 9 a.m. / finish / about 5 p.m. / hour's lunch break.

b)   ....

There be / lots / people / talk to / I enjoy play / records.

c)   ....

Yesterday / somebody ask / record / I not know.

d)   ....

The boss say / singer be very famous / — he call Louis Armstrong.

e)   ....

I like / songs / lot.

f) ....

I / write again soon.

g) ....

Love from Maya

15 MINUTES

3 *In this exercise, choose the word or phrase which best completes each sentence.*

1. I've been working here .... I was a young man.
   A when   B for   C since   D while

2. Great news! I've just been ....
   A promoted   B raised   C advanced   D put up

3. Her job is to .... the goods on the assembly line to make sure there are no defects.
   A secure   B guarantee   C check   D look

4. Workers who arrive late will be given three warnings and then ....
   A refused   B dismissed   C cancelled   D rejected

5. The job .... dealing with potentially dangerous situations. Are you still interested?
   A involves   B concerns   C offers   D encloses

6. Could you put me .... to your complaints department please?
   A on   B through   C in   D down

7. .... it was a very boring job, I worked hard and conscientiously.
   A In spite of   B However   C Despite   D Although

8. Most of the men went .... in protest at the cuts.
   A to strike   B in strike   C on strike   D at strike

9. I think I made a good .... at the interview.
   A appearance   B impression   C opinion   D idea

10. The chief engineer was in .... of nearly fifty men.
    A charge   B direction   C leadership   D management

11. Before long I was promoted to the .... of under-secretary.
    A job   B profession   C position   D vocation

12. .... I didn't lose my job. I was one of the lucky ones.
    A Unfortunately   B Fortunately
    C While   D Although

13 The company finally agreed to pay .... over £1,000,000 to those people they could no longer employ.
   A out   B off   C back   D in

14 Many women decided to .... their careers for their family life.
   A give up   B put down   C give in   D put up

15 They asked me if I had had any .... experience in this area.
   A before   B preliminary C early   D previous

16 Teachers find it difficult to .... on the small salaries they earn.
   A keep   B be   C alive   D survive

17 It was terrible – my best friend and I had both .... for the same job!
   A intended   B referred   C applied   D requested

18 My boss is so mean; he said that a pay rise was .... , and I've been working here for 20 years.
   A out of sight   B out of control
   C out of mind   D out of the question

19 After a long and bitter dispute, the two sides finally agreed to .... the problem.
   A decrease   B control   C discuss   D balance

20 I have an excellent job .... an architect's office.
   A by   B in   C with   D to

21 .... of the two candidates was suitable for the job.
   A No one   B None   C Neither   D Not any

22 How does this computer .... ?
   A go   B do   C run   D work

23 I'm sorry sir, there's .... in trying to contact him here – he was sacked over a month ago.
   A nowhere   B no way   C no point   D no idea

24 I'm on the dole now – I was .... by the dockyard when they started to lose money.
   A laid off   B put off   C called off   D sent off

25 She was a woman of great .... ; she was so good at her job that she soon rose to the top of the profession.
   A future   B ability   C opportunity   D possibility

Acknowledgements

Cartoons by Ben Rowdon

The publishers are grateful to the following for permission to reproduce copyright material:

Anthony Sheil Associates Ltd. for the extract from *The Growing Pains of Adrian Mole* by Sue Townsend © Sue Townsend 1982 (page 1); Judith Chernaik for the extracts from her book *Honor Thy Mother and Thy Father* (pages 5–6); Rover Group Ltd. for the use of the Rover 800 advertisement (pages 11–12); Innovations International Ltd. for the use of the Interplak advertisement (page 16); Innovations (Mail Order) Ltd. for the use of the Security Systems advertisements (page 20); Cambridge University Press for the extract from *Reading* by Frank Smith (pages 24–5); Heinemann Educational for the extract from *Teaching Reading Skills in a Foreign Language* by Christine Nuttall (pages 27–8); Tony Buzan for the extract from his book *Use Your Head* (pages 32–3 and 35); Weidenfeld and Nicolson Ltd. and Peters, Fraser and Dunlop for the extract from *The Middle Ground* by Margaret Drabble (page 37); Atheneum Publishers, an imprint of Macmillan Publishing Company, for the extract from *Miss Manners' Guide to Excruciatingly Correct Behaviour* by Judith Martin (pages 39–40); Domino's Pizza for the use of their advertisement (page 42); Oxford University Press for the extract from *Language Two* by Heidi Dulay, Marina Burt and Stephen Krashen © 1982 by Oxford University Press, Inc. Reprinted by permission (pages 46–7); Edward Arnold (Publishers) for the extract from *Linguistics in Language Teaching* by D. A. Wilkins (page 50); Heinemann Educational for the extracts from *Discover English* by Rod Bolitho and Brian Tomlinson (pages 53–5); Collins Harvill for the extract from *Arabia* by Jonathan Raban (pages 57–8); AA Publishing for the extract from *Walks and Tours in Britain* and Ordnance Survey for the use of the accompanying maps, © Crown copyright (page 67); Souvenir Press Ltd. for the extract from *Travelling Cat* by Frederick Harrison (pages 72–3); Virago Press for the extract from *The Short Stories of Willa Cather* by Willa Cather (page 78); Link House Advertising Periodicals for the use of the advertisements from *Exchange and Mart* (pages 80–1); Pelham Books for the extract from *Not There, Doctor*, © 1978, by Dr Robert D. Clifford (pages 85–6); Rodale Press, Inc. for the extracts from *Prevention* magazine, © 1991 Rodale Press, Inc., 33 East Minor Street, Emmaus, PA18098, all rights reserved; The Health Education Authority for the extract from the leaflet *The Most Common Disease in the World?* (page 92); The Department of Health for the use of the Nursing advertisement (page 100); Faber and Faber Ltd. for the extract from *A Taste for Death* by P. D. James (pages 103–4); Random House, Inc. for the extract from *Singin' and Swingin' and Gettin' Merry Like Christmas* by Maya Angelou, © 1976 by Maya Angelou (page 108)